D1328343

Across
the U.S.A.
--By Boat

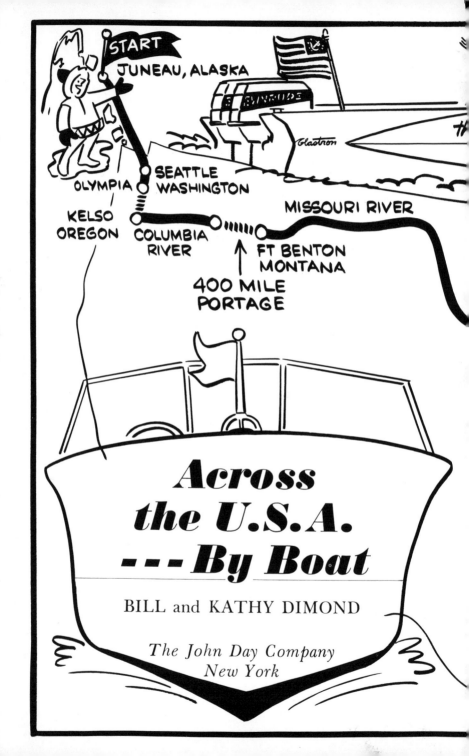

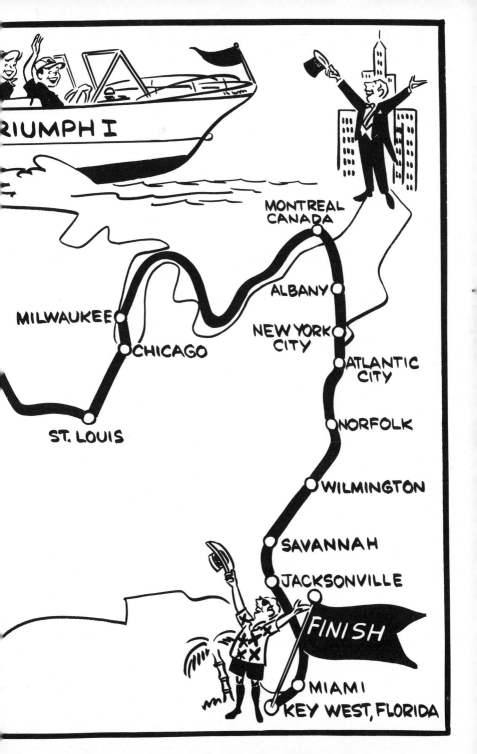

The John Day Company, 257 Park Avenue South, New York N.Y. an **Intext** publisher

Published on the same day in Canada by Longmans Canada Limited.

Library of Congress Catalogue Card Number: 71-109149
Printed in the United States of America

To
Robert N. West, Jr.,
who made the trip possible

Across the U.S.A. --By Boat

Columbus Never Had It So Good

Christopher Columbus may have had a better send-off, but I doubt it. My guess is that Columbus raised anchor and cleared port as quietly and modestly as possible. Who wants an audience when setting out to sail off the end of the flat world? As for me, William Dimond, lately of St. Louis and the trim, safe world of traveling salesmanship, there was no doubt that I was leaving all the flatness behind, and the question was whether I could shape up for what was ahead. I had exercised my best salesmanship on a goodly number of people, making them believe I could, and in the first-mate's seat next to me in the twenty-foot outboard sat my best vote of confidence, Kathy, my wife. Anyway, I said to myself while putting on my best please-the-press, please-the-sponsor smile, I'm that much one-up on Columbus. My wife is with me. Serves her right, too. She got us into this.

This flashback takes place at Juneau, Alaska, on June 10, 1968. Our destination was New York harbor, by way of the Alaskan intracoastal waterway, which is a shameless way of making a long stretch of unpredictable Pacific Ocean sound safe, and then on to the rivers and lakes of the continental United States and Canada. It would be an 8,500-mile boat ride, minus two early-on portages of about 400 miles in total. Those overland episodes are negligible. I will not apologize for them. God got here first and made the country the way it is, and if Kathy and I did not discover the Northwest Passage, we did negotiate a southerly version of it, and some passages that were not for sissies.

The negotiations were not all pleasure boating, although pleasure boating is what we were promoting for a well-known manufacturer of outboard motors. Pleasure, however, was not the key word in the adventure. The key word was Safety. The men in charge of the promotion planned a schedule for the trip. They told us before we set out that though it would be nice if we could adhere to the schedule, so that it would be easier to arrange press, radio, and television interviews and other plums of publicity, the schedule was at no time to take precedence over safety. The purpose, after all, was to prove that the trip could be made. To place the schedule ahead of, say, heeding a small-craft warning would be doing the company no favor.

There were two notable occasions when, as a good company man, Captain Dimond played it Captain Chicken. The occasions were about 6,000 water miles apart, in the Alaskan intracoastal at the outset, and on the East Coast's Intracoastal Waterway. Each time I had to console myself with "Well, you asked for it, Dimond." The second asking for it was the extension of the trip. We were the Juneau-to-New York boaters when we left Alaska. By the time we arrived in Milwaukee, where the sponsor's plant is located, we were the Juneau-to-Key West boaters.

Making the trip stretch as far as it could go, from the far northwest tip of the United States to the far southeast tip of it, was our idea. I do not recall the moment when the inspiration settled down in the cockpit of the *Triumph I* and wooed and won us. It may have been during one of the more idyllic stretches, when we were cruising the upper Missouri, making about ten sandbars an hour and wafting along through floating clouds of mosquitoes.

"Kathy, it may not be the right time to bring this up, but generally speaking, I'd say that boating beats working for a living."

"It does if you're named Ralph Evinrude. You're Bill Dimond, remember?"

"Well, what's wrong with being Boater Bill Dimond? What I'm building up to is to ask Ed Hanson if we can't

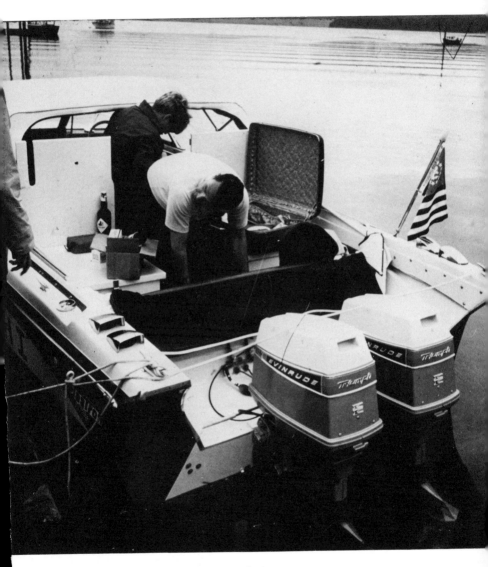

Our hectic departure from Juneau, Alaska.

push this trip on, go on to Key West with it instead of ending it in New York. Probably it wouldn't add more than a month, if that, to the time we'll be out."

I looked across the cockpit at her. She had been working on a major problem. Does mosquito repellent offset the antiburning properties of suntan oil? And if so, which is the less painful way to go, as a cinder or as a swollen lump of mosquito bites?

She said, "Big talk for a folding-door salesman who doesn't have a door to peddle anymore."

But she was grinning. Kathy is a girl with an eye for the far horizon, and I think that through the heat glare and the haze of mosquitoes she could see Key West more clearly than I could then. I couldn't see much beyond ten feet, which was our distance from the next friendly mudbank that would hang us up.

Ed Hanson, the public relations director for the sponsoring company, saw the Key West proposal as a logical extension of the trip as quickly as Kathy did. I acquired profound respect for the far-sighted Hanson vision, the Hanson thoughtfulness, the Hanson solicitude. I lost count of the times he anticipated our needs and the times he would ask, to mask his concern, as he popped up unexpectedly at some forlorn shore stop, "Hello, Kathy, Bill. How's your sex life?"

The ability to come up with a line that amuses the troops in the field is one of the marks of a good general. As for Hanson's question, the only fit companion for it was told me by a former Marine. He claimed that the commanding general of the San Diego recruit base during World War II would pause in front of a footsore, homesick recruit and ask the boot, "Son, is the mess hall serving you enough ice cream?"

The answer, of course, was "Sir, what's ice cream?"

We would not have known the pleasures of the Hanson heckling if Kathy had not been listening to the radio on a Saturday afternoon late in March. The Dimond household was operating that afternoon as a man's castle should, Kathy in the kitchen doing something elaborate with pots and pans, and me sacked out upstairs after a hard week in the folding-door business. She tuned in to "Welcome Aboard," a local broadcast on boating, by Sterling Harkins. It is believed by many boaters in the St. Louis area that Sterling cubbed under that noted Mississippi pilot, Mark Twain, but I know that that's not accurate. Twain was Sterling's apprentice. One or the other of us always listened to Harkins on Saturday afternoons to catch up on the week's gospel in boating. That Saturday the program included an announcement that a famous outboard-motor company was seeking a young couple, experienced in boating, to take a runabout from Alaska to New York. As Kathy listened, enthusiasm carried her away to the point that she abandoned her recipe, most unlike her, and ran upstairs to awaken me, a breach of Dimond discipline that she justified by telling me the details she had heard on the radio. I half-listened, said, "Whyoncha callem," and rolled over, which was showing more enthusiasm than the girl had really expected.

Sunday, Kathy continued her propaganda, and by evening I had agreed that it was worth writing to the sponsoring company. Monday morning, she decided that a letter would not do. Her haste could not wait on the United States mails. Sterling Harkins had mentioned Ed Hanson's name in the broadcast, so Kathy placed a call to Hanson's office in Milwaukee. A secretary there told Kathy that Mr. Hanson was not in but that she would send Kathy an application form for us to fill in. The secretary sounded as if she had been answering telephone calls from everyone who had ever tipped over a canoe and had thereby become a boating expert and the only logical choice for the trip.

More than eighteen hundred couples applied. When Hanson issued the first promotion message, he merely stated that the company was seeking "a young couple" and assumed that it would be understood he meant a man and woman properly wedlocked. So much for his innocence. He quickly revised the promotion message to read, "young married couple," which was an improvement but, like most screening devices, was not infallible. Some couples protested that any whippersnapper can be young, it requires no talent at all, and it is not until a man and wife have boated their way into Social Security that they are fit for such a journey.

A woman living on the eastern seaboard, and apparently ready to jump off the edge of it, wrote that she would be available, immediately, if the company would provide a baby-sitter for her ten children. She made no mention of allowing her husband to accompany her.

A lawyer presented splendid credentials. He also attached a rider: he must be allowed two months off every so often to handle his court cases.

Many letters were received from obviously well-qualified applicants who were ready to make the supreme sacrifice. There were two things that they all knew well: the joys of boating and the joys of bachelorhood. To a man, they were ready to grab a girl, any girl, anywhere, marry her, and be ready to start the trip if the company gave them the nod.

A few quick thinkers chose to try conquest from within the company walls. Several secretaries were approached with the same proposition: "Marry me, baby. With your connections we'll be a cinch to get the trip." All such proposals were refused. As a matchmaker, Hanson was a flop.

I have heard gossip that it was the expansive Hanson personality, enlarging itself during a gathering of the company's men on a cabin cruiser, that was responsible for the trip. Why not, said Hanson, saluting the sun as it did the decent thing and went over the yardarm, send a young couple on this gr-r-r-and adventure? Not pros, you understand, but no bathtub sailors either.

The original plan was to select one couple and have another on standby. Logic soon enough ruled that out. It was the logic of pride on both sides, the sponsor's and ours. The company, in its corporate wisdom, knew that it had to have faith in itself, in its ability to select two people who could go the distance. Kathy and I had to have our counterpart of that, faith in ourselves. I have played enough team games to resent having a substitute on the bench, hoping I will fumble and give him a chance to replace me on the field, though I admit that a sub's presence could stimulate my effort; but this was not a similar situation. Kathy and I were the team. No subs. All the way, or forfeit.

Without any coaching by us, the sponsors arrived at the same conclusion. One of the executives, I think it was Bob West, director of marketing, said, "Pick 'em, and then go all the way. Just be sure that they're people who won't quit unless the boat sinks, and then the thing's done with, anyway."

There were to be several occasions on open water when I wondered if Bob West had been speaking as a cool businessman or whether he kept a crystal ball hidden in his bottom desk-drawer.

The choice narrowed to four couples: husband-and-wife boaters from upper New York State, from Miami, from St. Petersburg, Florida, and us. Each of the four twosomes was invited to Milwaukee for an interview. The couple from New York State couldn't make it: local shortage of baby-sitters too acute at that time. We didn't have to plot our course around baby-sitters; we'll have to in time, but we didn't then.

I don't know what the considerations were with the couples from Florida. I do know that when we went to Milwaukee in late May, something was said about how nice it would be to have one of the man-woman crew be a professional photographer. That hurt me. Along with our certificates in navigation and boat handling, I had submitted samples of my work with a camera. I was certain that the man yearning for a boat driver who could take *Life* magazine cover photos on the side wasn't Matthew Brady or Robert Capa, and I thought some of the Say-Cheese stuff I'd made was good.

"What's wrong with my pictures?" I asked him. That was the finish of his objections. Probably he was afraid I would take a picture of him.

We were in Milwaukee being interviewed for three days. The interviews exhilarated Kathy. She said that she knew we would be chosen, that we had it. I didn't like the sound of "had it." When I had been a pilot with the Strategic Air Command, that little phrase had had a meaning quite different from what she optimistically meant by it.

When we got home to St. Louis, I immediately went out to Oklahoma City to address a sales meeting for several days, hoping to instill in some possibly doubting people the belief that folding doors are the salvation of the world. Just when I was believing it myself, Kathy called. As a news announcer she may not have style, but she gets the message across.

She said, "We got it—we got it—we got it!"

Lamely, I said, "Honey, I just got these guys all hopped up and I can't tell them I'm going to take off three months and drive a damn boat."

She said, "They've told me to go to the store tomorrow and pick out my outfits for the whole trip, when will you be home, tomorrow? We're supposed to leave for Seattle June third and we'll be in Juneau June fourth and the boat will be waiting for us there, gear and all, and do you think your last year's shorts will be okay?"

Well, that took care of her wardrobe and mine—and the folding-door business, too, when I called the boss. He said, "I can't talk now, Bill, better call me back." Two days later I did, and said that I didn't want to fold my doors behind me forever, just for a leave of absence.

He thought for a moment and then gave me an opinion.

Secretary of the Interior Walter J. Hickel, then governor of Alaska, bids us good-bye.

Just under way. Cruising outside of Juneau.

Obviously, it was not hastily arrived at. He had been thinking about it during those two days. He said in a kindly way,
trying to save me and my wife of less than four years from
my foolish self, "Bill, you're crazy."

We all receive stale news in different ways. My way was
to be silent. That was his way, too. We held the line open
silently until, as the man obliged to justify the company's
long-distance budget, he had to break the silence. He said
that "the West Coast thing, plus profit-sharing, is opening
up, and you're the man for it."

I had been saying that for some time. It was nice to hear
that I had been right. It was pleasant to think of what it
could mean to my mortgaged household in St. Louis
County, what the pleasures of the West Coast climate
could do for my frustrations as a Mississippi boater, swap-
ping the river waters full of beer cans, barges, pollution,
and Army Corps of Engineers locks for the blue Pacific.
Like stout Cortez, I was standing silent, on a dreamy peak
in Darien. Then, breaking that silence, I heard a voice—
mine', of all people's—saying, "I'm sorry. I'm still going to
take on this boating thing."

His reaction was that of a man with his hearing aid
turned off. Well, it is a good company, he is a good man.
Folding doors are grand for making a lot of cozy little
meeting rooms out of the grand ballroom of the Marshmallow Center Motel, or the other way around as the social
whirl demands, but suddenly I was otherwise committed.
I was a river rat. So help me, Mike Fink, here we come.

Brave thoughts, then. I wasn't so brave after the champagne send-off that introduced this chronicle. The champagne had been shared with the governor of Alaska, the
Honorable Walter J. Hickel, who has since gone on to
other duties in President Nixon's Cabinet as Secretary of
the Interior. He was proud of Alaska, proud that Juneau
was the starting point of this venture. Admittedly, it was
a commercial one. That is not a dirty word, "commercial."
The Phoenicians would not have set a sail if they had not

understood that word, and when I am an old Establishment grandfather, giving thanks for two boats on trailers in every driveway, I will recall with delight that the governor of Alaska and Joseph George, the mayor of Juneau, gave Kathy and me a champagne breakfast and sent us on our bumptious way, across the continental United States by water, on that morning of June 10, 1968.

I will also remember that small-craft warnings had been lifted just before we left, and that Kathy's eyes were misting as the water-police escort turned away from us when we hit the open waters of Auke Bay. And that I did not feel so Dimond-mighty confident, either. Aft, on the port, was fading Althaska, the Giant Land.

Ahead were the waters of the intracoastal. The night before, I had been reading a Coast Guard handbook, "Safety Notes for the Alaskan Fisherman—Dedicated in memory of all Alaskan fishermen who have lost their lives at sea."

Sometimes I read too much.

All the Gear That's Fit to Float

When the last escort boat dropped away, at about Middle Point, as we left Juneau, we felt like two children running away from home—mighty lonesome even before we were around the first bend. However, we had one advantage on any other runaways I've heard about. We were leaving in the family Cadillac, if General Motors and some other proud manufacturers will forgive me for mixing up my commercial metaphors.

Nature did not wait long to straighten me out on the mixing up of physical metaphors. The first nautical miles were about as smooth as the land miles on some Alaskan roads, just a light chop that reminds the neckbone it is connected to the tailbone. Kathy stored away the gear.

I stress the importance of the husband-and-wife relationship giving way to captain–first-mate relations when under way in a boat. It's "Aye-aye, sir" from her then. Upon docking, it may return to the more familiar "Yes, ma'am" from him. It's a system that worked well enough for whaling captains, and it did for us.

Kathy's work came to a halt when we rounded Douglas Island. The light chop gave way to building waves. Kathy lurched forward to the copilot's seat, a mix-up in terminology that I kept to myself and did not confess to her when she took the logbook in hand and said, "We pulled away at twenty minutes to twelve, right?"

"We did no such thing at no such time, Mrs. Dimond. We cast off and were under way at eleven-forty hours and you know it, and that is the kind of decent, seafaring, captain-respecting language you'll use in the log."

"Aye-aye, sir. What about when we get on the rivers?"

"Water's water, woman, some is salty and some is fresh, but we're not going to let little differences like that make the language of the log anything but one way—salty."

"Aye-aye, sir."

Well, that covers the marital courtesies, the admission that behind every good boater there stands a good wife. Now on to the lesser equipment, the manufactured and mechanical aids that equipped the boat. There cannot be a more sophisticated outboard floating anywhere, for private-owner pleasure. If there is, the man deserves the title of World's Prize Boating Nut for spending so much money when he could buy a larger bundle, a cabin cruiser, for the same number of dollars, or probably less. Consider the following list for cramming the most safety-luxury into the smallest boating space.

One Pierce-Simpson ship-to-shore radio. When it was first mentioned to me, I thought that it was overdoing it a bit to carry that sort of radio for cruising down rivers. On second thought, which took no time at all to come to me, I considered all the open water we would be crossing, and that radio was a pleasant thing to have at hand, just for the consoling presence of it—an electronic security blanket.

Pierce-Simpson radio direction finder. Dandy to have around if you get silly enough to have to use it. Fortunately, we didn't.

Danforth-White anchors, a ten-pounder with a 200-foot line and a six-pounder with a 100-foot line. The only thing I have against boating is the need for anchors. They are a chore. It is my theory that Noah got drunk on that mountaintop when his voyage finally ended, out of joy at never again having to put out an anchor.

Danforth-White Falcon horn. I intended to steal that at journey's end and keep it around the house for New Year's eves to come. It was a noble thought, but somehow it slipped my mind in Key West.

Corsair compass, Danforth-White.

Minolta camera. Good equipment, not for amateurs. Showing the color slides after the trip was completed, I seldom had to make excuses for such things as half the frame being a portrait of my thumb over the lens. I am still surprised that the *National Geographic* hasn't sent a man around, snooping on my techniques with a camera. Ah, well. It is the fate of some artists to go unappreciated in their lifetime.

Binoculars, by Zeiss. Wholesale, $75, by heavens.

Bilge pump, set of fenders, horn, by Peters and Russell. Naming the manufacturers is not altogether a matter of returning a favor by free advertising. The gear was excellent, and we are grateful.

A tent, two sleeping bags, a lantern, a two-burner stove, a one-burner stove, and a thermal heater—all by Coleman. Now, that is a tradename I have known since Boy Scout age. We did not use the tent. We did make frequent use of the stoves, the lantern, and the sleeping bags, which unfortunately were also Boy Scout models. Single occupancy.

We had a Coleman cooler and a jug. The cooler was big enough to hold a case and a half of canned beer and enough ice to keep it cold. We set out in style, with the beer on glacier ice—a durable commodity. It endured for five days, and that, of course, is a tribute to the cooler, but also a measure of the endurance of glaciers, the talent they have for hanging on. Glacier ice is equally remarkable for its property of hanging over. During the week we spent in Juneau, making practice runs with *Triumph I,* sight-seeing glaciers, posing for publicity photos, getting outfitted, the busy days were inevitably followed by parties. At most of those events, full of hospitality as only Alaskans seem to be hospitable—great warmth in a snow-and-ice background—the drinks were cooled with glacier ice. Nowhere have I met ice that stayed ice in my system overnight and the next morning held my head in a firm and frozen, blinding bind. I suggest to anyone planning to visit Alaska that he accept the glorious hospitality but decline, in the interest of self-preservation, the glacier ice.

Camp kit and cooking utensils, by Mirro Aluminum. The cooking set consisted of seven pieces, of which each was a little smaller than the next in order of succession, and the housewife's term for that, said Kathy, is "nesting." Somehow, the term struck me as inaccurate and ludicrous, but women seem to like it and in the thirty or so nights we spent on board the boat, when nightfall found us with only a mudbank available for a marina, we were glad to have that nest of cookingware aboard. I never did learn if the utensils had gourmet possibilities. Kathy's shipboard cooking was endlessly committed to canned ravioli and canned spaghetti. I had to drive a boat from Juneau to Key West to discover that my wife is, in her cooking heart, a canned Italian. We also had a coffeepot. Kathy used it every morning. Her coffee is not Italian. It is pure Wyoming cowboy, and I like it that way.

We had on board a first aid kit, Johnson & Johnson; spark plugs, Champion; four Stearns life jackets; a logbook, meaning two Spiral notebooks, the deluxe seventy-nine-cent models that are favored by apple-polishing students because they are big and make the teacher think every priceless word of his is being taken down; an Eveready flashlight and a set of flares made by Olin, a distress signal that I several times thought of sending up in the hope that some St. Bernard would come rushing to my rescue with a martini, but didn't; an Ansul fire extinguisher; a set of tools; a Gerber knife, in case I had to skin a bear; a rifle, in case I had to shoo a bear out of the beer cooler; and a paddle. The paddle was the last thing put on board, at Juneau. I do not know whose afterthought that was. I do know that it was presented us with fine corporate coolness on the part of some company man or another, and nobody made an up-the-creek comment, which we took as conclusive evidence that we were dealing with serious, adult persons and that however much fun this trip

I check out our electronic security blanket, the ship-to-shore radiotelephone.

Kathy testing our sleeping gear. The seat on the right also folds down to make a comfortable bunk-setting.

might be, it was not *basically* a lark. It was actually magnani-
mous of the company man to throw in a paddle. Much
earlier, spare propellers had been stored in the boat. Any
skipper, no matter how able, can lose a wheel to debris,
and having spares aboard was as elementary good sense
as a spare tire on the family car. But the paddle was a
company-given security, of sorts, against both engines
conking out. Now, that required some humility on the part
of the company, and I was grateful for the paternal solicitude it represented. I'm also grateful that it was an unwar-
ranted addition. Both engines were good for the distance.
One gave me trouble, about midway, but that was my fault.
The poor thing tried to tell me it needed help, and I did
not get the message, simple though it was. But more of
that later.

The boat's outfitting was thorough and expensive. The
Dimonds' outfitting was thorough and not so expensive,
though it looked good on Kathy, and all of it fit into our
two overnighter bags. We had ski parkas for the run
through the Alaskan waters. The Dimond wardrobes
thereafter were wash-and-dry shorts and shirts. Kathy became the leading authority of the North American conti-
nent on the subject of riverside Laundromats, or the
absence of them. It is my contention that we made the trip
on a laundry-cycling schedule, not a sailing schedule. It is
her contention that the United States will not be safe for
boating until there are washers and driers at every fifty-
mile interval on all navigable waters. The company's office
of public relations in Milwaukee kept a map on a wall, with
pins noting our stop-by-stop progress, and never did they
know that those markers should have been clothespins.

The clinching convenience in the *Triumph I* was a feature
that neither of us appreciated at first sight. It was a piece
of carpentry—two chests constructed aft, matching on
port and starboard. They were three feet deep, two feet
wide, four feet long. The tops were double-hinged at the
middle and angled so that the seats, forward at the wheel,

could be let down to join the cabinet tops and make a comfortable bunk-setting for our sleeping bags. We thought the lockers a nuisance when they were proposed and installed. The first night we couldn't find a roof ashore, we thought them the finest contribution to man's and woman's comfort since the invention of back scratching.

Finally, in my wallet there was the most important outfitting—credit cards. I don't know how Magellan got around the world without them.

Curious Creature, the Killer Whale

In Kathy's log for the day we arrived at Juneau for the week-long training period, there is the remark "We all giggled a lot." It closes the day, at a party. The next day the log records that we met the *Triumph I* and in Kathy's scrambling about the boat, introducing herself to it, within the first two minutes she "broke two fingernails."

She did not know it, but within twelve hours or so she had experienced the essences of the trip, a lot of giggles and some broken fingernails. Giggles are girlish—a man must accept them with the other benefits of the sex—but wails over broken fingernails can be deafening. Physically, the fingernails were the most severe damage we had. That was partly luck; no amount of preparation, intelligence, and cunning outweighs good luck. When I have planned something well and the plan works flawlessly, I tell myself, "You were lucky, Dimond." Keeps me from getting over-confident, which is the sudden death of good luck.

Now back to the matter of our leaving Juneau in that splendor of equipment, the *Triumph I,* and having the escort boats fall behind, and the seas pick up and introduce us to the feeling of being lonesome. Less than an hour before, we had been made members of the Royal Order of the Walrus ("Do you have a clean mind?" "You bet your sweet Oosik I do"), and it was beginning to dawn on me that we were the only walruses in these waters at the time. All the others, being of sound mind, were tucked in by a nice shoreline at a walrus bar. By 1330 we'd had it. We pulled to Taku Harbor, out of the mean chop of the south-westerlies onto the land, where the early June sun had some warmth, even in Alaska.

We had made only thirty-four miles, and the long northern daylight would allow us to push on if the wind and the seas calmed in the afternoon. We said as much to a fisherman, and without bothering to wet a finger and lift it to the wind, or otherwise consult science, he told us to forget about it and sit with him on the dock and hear fish stories the rest of the day. It would be a much better day for well-spun stories than for putting out to the open waters, he said, and speaking of stories, that reminded him we had not met Tiger Olsen.

And so we met Tiger Olsen. It will remain one of the bonuses of our lives that the wind was kicking as it was that day and that instead of pressing on to Petersburg, as the schedule would have had us do, we stayed in Taku Harbor and learned from Tiger that it is the hub of the spiritual universe. Tokyo, New York, and London, and probably Marshmallow Center, Iowa, have heavier traffic through town than Taku Harbor does, but those other hamlets are keeping a head count only of the living. (Tiger supposes that it pleases their chambers of commerce, and they brag a lot about the volume of business the tourists bring. He doesn't keep score in that commercial, selfish fashion.) Tiger reckons the traffic through Taku Harbor in souls, clean and happy and eager souls, passing through Taku Harbor en route to their eternal rewards.

"Everybody who dies," he said, "has to come through here first, on their way to heaven, and they do it, too, no way around it, you know."

He fixed Kathy, and then me, with a serene and knowing look, an Alaska-given certainty behind it that we could not doubt or question the truth of what he was saying. We couldn't, either, and of course we didn't refuse when Tiger offered to show us about the dock area and explain the simplicity of life at heaven's gateway. Tiger lives by his catches in the water. He looked at our boat and allowed that she was handsome and that she'd be just as handsome in the morning as she was then if someone had the good sense to moor her to the lee side of the dock. He did that while I blushed. Thought I'd forgotten how to blush. He showed Kathy a crab, a live and scuttling one. She had never seen one before and she rewarded Tiger with a squeal.

Then he told us that he was not feeling well but that an airplane would be landing soon, an amphibian, and would take him to Juneau.

"Oh, you call them up on the radio, or a phone or what?" I asked him. Straight-man Dimond. I was the delight of the summer tourist season for Tiger Olsen.

"Nope. Didn't call anyone. But they'll be here, about another hour."

"Tiger, I don't—Oh, I see. Come here every week at this time. That's it."

"No, that's not it. But they'll be by. I know."

I was going further into the matter. He was sounding a touch too much New England to me—Silas the town wit sitting on a cracker barrel and taking down the city slicker who was innocently asking directions and getting run around the down-home Yankee's barn for the amusement of the native donkeys. Kathy saved me. She put a strong elbow in my ribs and said she knew Mr. Olsen would be well taken care of in Juneau and that she was certain the airplane would arrive promptly, so could he give us some more details on his hometown's unusual advantages? He could.

"They don't just flock through here, like a mile-wide spread of migrating geese, those folks going to heaven," he told us. "That wouldn't look right, would it? No, it's an orderly procession and a real polite company, no shoving, you know, and everyone friendly, like they've all the time in the world to get where they're going, but it's not an advertised route. I know the pass they go through and many of the spirits talk to me on the way through. Oh, you meet a strange one now and then; one was a raven, big as a man, and I had doubts about a raven's chances of getting

Tiger Olsen and an Alaskan fisherman showing Kathy two fresh-caught Dungeness crabs.

into heaven, but it was all right, turned out he was an Indian and you know they can be independent; if he wanted to go in as a raven it must have been all right, had prior clearance, you know. And that's how I know the airplane will be coming, in fact it's almost here now. I talked with the spirits and asked them to send an airplane and take me up to the doctor. I'd better have supper, just barely got time. You folks come along with me."

We went along with him, and he prepared his modest supper, a warming-over process, and was just comfortably seated and spooning it up when there was the sound of an airplane coming in. Tiger Olsen looked up, somewhat exasperated. He said, "By gosh, the spirits might have told them to give me time for supper."

The pilot and a man with him came up from the dock to Olsen's, saying they had come in from the back country and had decided to set down for a coffee break and a visit, and how were things with their favorite Tiger? Tiger said things were well, considering, but that he had been feeling poorly and would appreciate a lift to Juneau. The pilots were solicitous and suggested immediate departure. Tiger told us good-bye, and the glance he gave us, smiling but sharp, suggested that Alaska is no place for spirit doubters.

Later, but not much later, I tried to raise Juneau by radio on the *Triumph*. The fisherman who had started it all by introducing us to Tiger Olsen told me to never mind the radio. "Dead area here today," he said. "Couldn't raise a ghost." Ghosts again, I thought. We stayed the night on the *Triumph*. Kathy slept soundly. I didn't. I woke frequently, listening to the wind, wondering what it was trying to tell me about tomorrow's weather, trying to get my two-Boy-Scouts-sized rump settled into that one-Boy-Scout sleeping bag and wondering if I would come this way again. As a raven?

I woke up as a man, recognizable to my wife as Bill Dimond by the precoffee snarling, which was somewhat more mellow than usual because of the glory of the dawn. It was another Alaska amazement to me that five o'clock in the morning could be beautiful. It never happened in the folding-door business. We had the coffee and discussed the roof of the *Triumph.* It is a roadster boat. The folding top goes down by hand and is supported by braces, and it must be coaxed and spoken to lovingly. I suppose those procedures are a delight to automobile lovers who specialize in MG-TD's and Morgans and such esoteric museum pieces, but in heavy waves and in rain there was more water coming in through the *Triumph*'s overhead than was necessary for baptizing us as transcontinental voyagers. We did not put down the top this morning, of course. Not formally, anyway. No need to. The water found its way in, easily as Tiger's spirits, but a lot colder. Damned colder. Fixing that tarp, or canvas, or sieve, was going to be my first order of business in Petersburg, ninety miles distant, and we set out in the heavy waves.

We were not a half hour out before we acquired our second escort group. Killer whales. I liked the escort out of Juneau better but had to admit that for loyalty this one had it all over the politicians, boat salesmen, the Chamber of Commerce, and the Coast Guard. This school of killer whales took an instant liking to us. We could tell it by the playful rolls they made, the better to show us their cavity-free teeth, and the effortless way they went along at half throttle, keeping up with our 20-to-25-knot speed. They were going to make it up to us for the fact that Alaskan hospitality, grand as it is on land, had turned back at the harbor's mouth and not shared the open water with strangers.

A killer whale is not a whale of a whale. It is, in fact, a kind of porpoise. I would estimate that if two sharks, maybe three if the story is to be stretched—but not by much—were dismantled and reassembled into one terrifying machine, that would be an easy enough method of

The first of our killer-whale escorts surfaces off our bow.

fashioning a killer whale. Assuming that there wasn't one available and for some insane reason one was on order.

I knew of killer whales as I know of presidents and movie stars and Jackie Kennedy Onassis, by pictures and by tall tales told. In the Air Force I was a peaceful copilot of a B-47. However, it was a line of business that left one at the mercy of moulting eagles, old flyers who had done hangar time with Eddie Rickenbacker or Joe Foss. It was a man of the Foss vintage, World War II Marine Corps aviation, who told me of the relative viciousness of perils that take to the sea.

"We was on antisubmarine patrol," he began. (You must forgive the plural pronoun, the singular verb. Marines always think of themselves as singular, and I have been waiting years to get in that punitive pun.) Anyway, they was on antisubmarine patrol, a flight of Grumman torpedo bombers. He was the section leader, and after some three hours of wasting time over the Pacific's lovely boondocks, he took a heading home to the carrier. As he banked, he saw a black-blue shape in the water. He signaled the attack. That is how the Marine Corps, that valiant day, kept the world safe for democracy by blasting one loner of a killer whale out of the water, straight up into a water spout of eternity, with some thousands of dollars' worth of the taxpayers' bombs. He told it, that former Marine, as an accomplishment worthy to be inserted in a prominent place on the Sistine Chapel ceiling, at the expense of erasing several leading angels if necessary.

He disgusted me at the time. My killer instincts are those of a fly at the business end of a swatter. I do not believe that the balance of nature is much benefited by a flight of torpedo bombers engaging in combat with a solo killer whale. However, on this high-seas, sieve-topped, skittering morning off Alaska it would have been a delight to my pacifist nature to have had those killer whales peel off and take their loving attentions elsewhere.

They did not. They saw us right to the gates of Petersburg, and when we reported their escorting ways, the story was picked up by news services, radio, and television. For the next four months those killer whales were always with us in interviews. They were harmless, really, and I would have liked to give them a better press, but the press would not permit it. Reporters, fresh from being sent out on assignment by an editor, appreciate the deadliest of the species and will embrace a killer whale as something that, on the basis of kinship, will impress an editor as a story.

Perhaps there was danger in those killer whales if we had slowed or lost our engines or in any way indicated that our twenty-foot length was not as powerful as was theirs. However, at this safe distance, I prefer to think that they were curious and gregarious, and for all I know were accompanying us as decoys, in event a superannuated Marine fly-bomber spotted us on that choppy surface, defenseless.

Alaska, the Giant Land

The Indian word for it is Althaska, the Giant Land. The land is also gigantic in hospitality, and that is not a sign of selective senility on my part; I am aware I have said it before. So now for a word on hospitality as it is practiced in these truly united states, no matter how they may appear to be coming apart at the sectional seams from one headline to the next.

Alaska is our last frontier. That is a rather trite statement, and I will take the triteness out of it by claiming that the hospitality we found in Alaska is something that has been imported from the continental United States and made larger, in the specific and individual doses, because the land is so big and lonesome. I mean, where the Alaskan land itself is such an overstatement, sentiment and hospitality must be in perspective to the horizon, and that seems to go heaven-high. Kathy and I were seeing Alaska for the first time, and as natives of the crammed county of St. Louis, we found everything from people to skyline marvelously open. Then, I recalled the kindness shown by natives of the Ozarks to city innocents stranded on a back road by an asthmatic automobile, and the conclusion we made was that the people of Alaska just brought to their Giant Land the leftover frontier hospitality of the mainland United States, and that we have more of it still in residence than newspapers and television newscasts would lead us to believe. It is a happy thought that I found growing on me, long after Alaska, and by the time we reached Key West, I believe it was our credo for life. However, it is a belief that required more than thirty years to acquire, and it *began* in Alaska.

Our run from Tiger Olsen's gateway-to-the-hereafter to Petersburg covered ninety miles and required five hours. The swells were not much less ambitious than they had been the day before, but we felt an obligation to the company schedule, an obligation made stronger by our inability to make radio contact. I had visions of the factory in Milwaukee collapsing under the thunderous force of mass-executive apoplexy as twenty vice-presidents pressed self-destruct buttons to celebrate the failure of the Great Mission on its first day out. Bless them, we learned they *had* been worried, and for us, not for the company name.

Coming in to Petersburg, we were met by a Coast Guard cutter, the *Elderberry*. When I was able to read its name—and the way the seas were running that almost required running the *Triumph* up the *Elderberry*'s fantail—I had high hopes for the *Elderberry*'s brand of Coast-Guard–Alaskan hospitality. I might as well have expected horse racing on the U.S.S. *Saratoga*. There was no wine on the *Elderberry*, it was all squared-away Coast Guard, and when they took us in tow, the crew of the *Elderberry* defrosted us with black coffee, the standard grog of all American ocean vessels. I have had sufficient contact with the United States Navy, the Coast Guard, and civilian ships at sea and on the Mississippi, to marvel that 90 percent of the world is still salt and fresh water, and not caffein-loaded. However, Kathy and I agreed that the Coast Guard coffee, off Petersburg that cold morning, was worth double its weight in martinis.

The pride of Petersburg is its fisheries, and we toured them. Oil may be Alaska's future. Probably it is. That is a pity. First its future was gold. Then it was fish. Kathy thinks gold is prettier than fish. I think fishing fleets are prettier than oil rigs. As for smell, I'll take gold every time, over either oil or fish. We were a disappointment to the fishery people. They asked us if we needed provisions, but we did not. If we had, it would have been salmon to the scuppers

Hefting a 42-pound king salmon, which I caught trolling from the *Triumph I.*

for the *Triumph.* All around, we were a disappointment to the good people of Petersburg, both to the fisheries and to Bob Thorstenson, a company dealer. Thorstenson would have been delighted to supply us with something the company top brass had forgotten, a motor maybe, or a steering wheel, but the one thing that had not been supplied us that we needed was an ashtray, the dash-mounted model. We got two of them. Why it took us another thousand miles to think of getting a dash-mounted holder for soda or beer cans, I do not know. I like to think, however, that Lord Nelson occasionally slipped up, too.

Thorstenson and Art Hammer, also a company dealer (boating is another latter-day gold field in Alaska) took us out to lunch. In the glacier fields. Hammer's wife packed a lunch and we paid a call on the Le Conte Glacier. Now, I know that statistics can mislead. Again, in the words of my favorite riverman, Mark Twain, there are lies, damn lies, and statistics. I must solemnly offer, however, that there is sufficient ice in the Le Conte Glacier to refrigerate New York City, freeze it solid in July and hold it that way through August of the next year, and that is not a bad idea, either.

But it is not clean ice. Glaciers are not discriminating. They slide down over the real estate and take along with them whatever strikes their fancy. Glaciers are wolfish that way.

We wandered, during that lunch, among the ice packs of debris broken away from the glacier as it made its way to the open water, and were introduced again to a terrifying fact of life with glacier chunks. They turn over in their sleep when they hit that nice, warm, dozing water of some thirty-five degrees. Alaskan children sometimes swim, or wade, anyway, in water of such summery Alaskan tempera-ture, but they stay awake while doing it. Glacier chunks don't. They float along, not looking where they are going and not expecting company, and if a motorboat such as the *Triumph* comes too close and startles the ice chunk, it will rouse suddenly and flip over. That is a literal truth. It is also a literal truth that a glacier chunk is a baby iceberg and the portion of it that shows is a small part of the mass beneath the water. So the danger of flipping one, by disturbing its rest with the wake of the *Triumph,* coming in too close, was considerably on our minds. Fortunately for Thorstenson and Hammer, we told them that we had had several valuable schoolings. The company had put us through a three-day education in their motors at Milwaukee, en route to Alaska, and at Juneau we had been taken into glacier fields and taught respect for ice. Kathy and I were better prepared than the captain of the *Titanic.*

And after all that, while I was greedily grabbing for the last of Mrs. Hammer's fried chicken, there was a magnificent icy-holocaust heaving of a glacier chunk. Do not quarrel with the language. The damned thing was off our port quarter, perhaps an eighth of a mile away, and it turned turtle, gave a great and frightening and, considering its bulk, ludicrous upside-downing of itself. I do not think it was the effect of the *Triumph*'s wake. That chunk of iceberg simply woke up, saw that it had an audience, and chose to perform. If it could have swamped us, or better yet have landed topside-down on us, it would have been a pleased mountain of ice, but it was a novice at trapping tourists, and sprung its trick too soon, so all it got for its effort were gasps and gulps and gratitude that I was not sufficiently distracted by its performance to miss my grab for the last piece of chicken. The morsel of chicken was still warm. Kathy and I have both been instructed in the justices of a fiery hell for all who do not boat and live according to the rules, and we accept the teaching, but after our time in the Giant Land, my faith is wavering in one regard: A proper hell, a punitive and unforgiving hell, is one made not of fire, but of ice. Some air-conditioning salesman is bound to go to hell and make a fortune there, but I cannot imagine a heating salesman who could succeed in making gla-

ciers or their offspring livable. Usually, it is not wise for
a man writing about a given subject to refer the reader to
another writer who has done it better, but on the matter
of the relative horrors and blessings of cold and of fire, I
recommend "To Build a Fire," by Jack London. He'd do
the same for me if he came back in an outboard.

From Petersburg and its acrobatic ice, we went through
the Wrangell Narrows. They are narrow, riverlike, and we
did not have charts. That is amazing. Nobody had thought
of charts for the Narrows, though we had sufficient charts
to paper the White House. The Narrows can be defeating.
A wrong turn leads to a dead end, and nowhere a traffic
cop or a friendly service station, but with the good luck
that favors the clean-living chartless we made it to Wrangell. Where there were no hotel rooms available. I thought
it nice of Wrangell to have a hotel, even if there were no
rooms empty. There is a fine, civilized sound to "No Va-
cancy." I was reconciled to *Triumph* celibacy, another night
on the boat, but the boat dealer in Wrangell, Dan Roberts,
said he had a friend who had a water-side cabin, and we
were welcome to it. He said it had the ultimate Alaskan
luxury—hot water—and that settled the matter for Kathy.
She had hair-washing to do, and wash her blonde crown
she did, but all the heat in that cabin was in the water. It
would have been warmer, in the sack, on the boat. June 11
in Alaska is no kin to that date in, say, Iowa.

Waves Do Not Make for Comfort

We slept until 0930, in that cold cabin at Wrangell. We had left word for an early call, but the considerate hosts looked at the dawning day, decided the early portion of it was not fit for boating, and did not arouse us. We had done 165 miles the day before, rough mileage, so we appreciated the sleep and the offer to delay more boating by a tour of the town of Wrangell. Enthusiasm? You would think that Kathy and I had never seen a fish or an Alaskan fishery or a lumberyard before, and would be content to sit there and rust away the balance of our lives. I could have stayed the day at the lumberyard. I am, as a child of the twentieth century, accustomed to what man does with steel and other hard goods, but the wonders of dealing with raw trees, from paper pulp to my former love, folding doors, awes me. Anyway, it was rainy and foggy, and I had not yet been able to make the *Triumph I* roof function as anything better than a shower nozzle.

But by 1300 the water was calm, and though there was rain and fog and the *Triumph* welcomed both aboard, smooth water could not be rejected, so we left Wrangell. We were immediately back in the paper industry. The water was log-ridden. I had thought that the Mississippi River in springtime was the champion of the solid-wood river league. We drove sixty-six miles, or logged sixty-six miles, to Meyers Chuck, through water below us in the honest form of ocean and what we were now convinced was the hellish counterfeit of water in the shape of rain and fog above us, alongside us, and wettest of all, smack in the boat with us. I had worked on that overhead every night since leaving Juneau and had tried every solution except bubble gum. If my jaws had not been so weary cursing the tarp's porousness, I would have given the gum a try.

We took a breather—meaning a can of beer apiece—at Meyers Chuck and then had a meeting of the crew. Our crew meetings were weighted, as the saying goes in business circles. Kathy said, "Let's stay here. We've gone sixty-six miles and my hair is wrecked." She weighs 118 pounds.

I said, "It's thirty-five miles to Ketchikan, it doesn't look like worse water to me, there is a motel there and they have a room open for us according to what I hear on the radio, and your hair won't look any worse thirty-five miles from now than it does here."

My weight is 200. That is, after jogging. I did not jog while boating. So my weight was more. And I threw it around on board the *Triumph I,* the little boat that would not quit. We went on to Ketchikan. Kathy was grateful. We pulled up to an aircraft float, had the boat pulled from the water, had ourselves pulled to a motel, and Kathy was asleep in two seconds flat, by her own admission in the log. I could not contest the timing. My falling-asleep time on this night, as on virtually every other night, was instantaneous. It will occur to many people that our pace was leisurely, that we frequently dodged mileage we could have made, but I must make the defensive statement that we did what we safely could, that we were obliged to be young and think old, or conservatively, that we had to weigh our strength against our good judgment, and if that sounds stuffy, so be it. A lot of nonstuffy sailors are asleep in the deep, ahead of their time, and Bill Dimond doesn't want to join their second-guessing company.

We stayed a day in Ketchikan. The weather was an Alaskan bonus. We should have taken to the water, but we did not, and we had a promotional excuse. We were to be interviewed on television. The interviewer did not show up. Two newspaper reporters did, but they were not the convenience to me that the no-show television man became. The day of beautiful weather in Ketchikan was followed by much treachery on the part of the weather, and it took us eleven days to beat our way to Seattle, the first big port of call and of scheduled fuss-making. Those eleven days are worth some detailing, and I might as well blame the difficulties we had on the absent television man. Somebody has to take responsibility for the weather, and he isn't here to defend himself.

Anyway, by 1100 on June 14 we decided that the channel out of Ketchikan was about as livable for a small boat as it was going to get, so we put out. We were under way about an hour, passing the Twin Islands, when the antenna allowed that the waves were too much for it and fell off. I screwed it back in place while Kathy fought the wheel and learned what back muscles are all about. The antenna almost immediately fell off again. I do enjoy sane equipment. That antenna had decided it was all right for us to be crazy and take the pounding of the waves, but it would not. So I did the sporting thing and did not put it up a third time, but lashed it to the side of the *Triumph*. It rattled along contentedly, and I did not again hoist it in rough waters. Others shared the antenna's judgment of the roughness of the day, because a Coast Guard helicopter came overhead, checking our progress, and we signaled that it was satisfactory. Not comfortable, but right side up.

We made eighty-seven miles that day, to a berth at the Prince Rupert Rowing and Yacht Club. We came in by way of Chatham Sound, which is Canadian water, and the Dominions welcomed us by having the waters smooth at the Dixon Entrance. The welcome trailed off abruptly into more waves, compounded by the difficulties of harbor navigation. I had become too salty too fast with my success at open-water navigation. Harbor navigation was another matter, as I said to myself when I got lost coming in to Prince Rupert, an embarrassment that was not lost on Kathy. When she asked, "Why are you following that fishing boat?" I said, "Why, it seems the friendly thing to do. Doesn't everybody?" She never brought it up again, and it is just as well because I still haven't a better answer.

The fifteenth was another of those days that inspired me to work on the tarp roof of the *Triumph*. I laid on a mile or so of waterproof tape, bought provisions, and accepted some gifts of salmon. The *Triumph*'s salmon inventory at that point was thirty pounds. In conversation about the trip, I notice that Kathy and I both talk about the Alaska portion of it more than any other, but despite our fascination with things Alaskan, neither of us has quite recovered the fondness for salmon that we once had.

June 15 did not have a dawn. The fog just became a little less black, with some gray shot through it, and the rain was just a little less solid than the open water. Splendid day for testing the latest roof work, and it did turn out to be improved. Kathy tried the impossible, to keep the inside of the windshield free of fog, and I made a command decision to settle for Namu as the night's docking.

Namu is a cannery town, and the season wasn't open, so the population was down to the hard core, about two dozen. It looked like the center of the civilized world to us because as we pulled in the sun showed itself. We were back in the world of light again, and we agreed that tomorrow would be splendid. Namu itself was splendid that late afternoon and evening, with the charm of boardwalks about the harbor and a backdrop of a clear small river and a lake set back in the hills. That country is God's own stage design, of course, and a man should expect nothing but the best from such a source, yet the perfection of it never ceased to awe us.

We made up the *Triumph* staterooms, one sleeping bag each, port and starboard, and turned in at 2015 hours, practically late afternoon at that time of year in the north. We dined sumptuously as always when eating on board— spaghetti and crackers. We used the crackers to spoon up the spaghetti. There are two matters of equipment that I did not go into, discussing the marvelous outfitting of the

The fishing settlement of Namu,
British Columbia.

Fixing dinner at Namu.

Triumph I. We had a tree saw on board. The tree saw, in the natural order of shipboard stowage—important things on top of the storage chests—sank down to the very bottom. I recall seeing it come aboard, and thinking that it would be a sorry finish to the adventure if we ever became so stranded and lost and forlorn as to have to use the tree saw and build a house, awaiting rescue.

The second equipment left unmentioned was tableware. That's because we didn't have any. So it was either spoon up spaghetti with crackers or saw it up. There is an excellent cafeteria at Namu, but Kathy was too shy to beg a fork, I was too proud to steal, and we were getting handy with crackers, anyway.

June 17 was a grand day. We left Namu Harbor with boastful promises, captain to crew, of equaling the 210 miles we had made the day we crossed to Namu. Such talk was the undoing of the port engine. It began to race, out of gear, and the best Air Force language I had available would not convince that engine to settle down. I put it on tilt, out of the water and shut down, and gave praise to the genius who had designed this as a two-engine voyage. I diagnosed it as an ailing lower unit and made for Finn Harbor. Beautiful place. I hope to see it again, on two engines. At Finn Harbor, we were advised to go on to Dawson Landing, for the convenience of having parts flown in. The advice was good but the necessity disheartening. That day of sunshine and calm was made for one purpose—to get us across the seventy miles of Queen Charlotte Sound in unusual smoothness. I couldn't, or wouldn't, try it on one engine.

Dawson Landing provided. I radioed Bryant's Marine in Seattle, and the doctor there, Dick Sharp, agreed with me that it sounded like lower-unit trouble and that he would have a replacement in the air at once. That was about 1400, and I gave the first mate time off to go see the natural wonders of Dawson Landing, which are considerable. She went with an outstanding local guide, Billy, the grandson

A friendly deer at Dawson Landing, British Columbia.

of John Dragvik, a retired fisherman. At the edge of the forest that surrounds Dawson Landing, Billy introduced Kathy to two deer. The deer came within twenty feet of them, posed for a photograph, and altogether cemented Kathy's belief that the grand and great Northwest is the Garden of Eden put back in working order, and an improvement on the original.

Meanwhile, I was at the general store, asking foolish questions of the owner, Lucky Backen. For instance, I asked him if he had charts of the area. He said he didn't. No call for them, everybody knows those waters, back-of-their-hands sailing. Plainly, it would serve nothing to be rude to Lucky and point out that I wasn't Everybody, and the back of my hand is a navigational aid I've tried a time or two before, with no success. By the time Kathy and her guide, Billy, returned, chattering of lovable deer, it was getting on in the afternoon and Dawson Landing began betting on whether or not the city slickers in Seattle would get through that day with the repair parts. Just when the odds had reached the longest, with all of Dawson Landing, and Kathy Dimond as an honorary citizen of it, voting against Bill Dimond, who was keeping his faith in city slickers, there was the sound of an aircraft engine. In came Sharp, from Seattle. He had played it safe. He brought a lower unit. He also brought an engine. We played it square. The lower unit was the culprit, and we replaced it quickly. We were set for the next day.

We were also set for the next hundred-plus nights, whenever we dined in the *Triumph* saloon. Kathy bought flatware at Lucky's.

The morning of the eighteenth was splendid on the engine front, and miserable on the weather. We were still lagging a day behind the good weather, and I was building a stronger case against the one-day delay that started it all, our wait for the television interview that never took place. We were up at 0630, and at 0800 decided the water would not improve. So we accepted the weather on its own terms and ventured forth. I put up with its terms for about an hour, then headed for Duncanby Landing. A large motor yacht, the *Chiquita III,* was moored there and was to make the crossing that afternoon. She set out at 1500 and a half hour later radioed me, with the voice at the transmitter bobbing up and down with the waves, to stay right where we were. We did.

On the morning of the nineteenth we were up at 0600, giving praise to the sunshine, and within fifteen minutes were headed for the Sound. Before we were into it, it became obvious that the twenty-foot *Triumph* was hopelessly overmatched. The waves were running ten to twelve feet. It would have been healthier, and the chances of survival better, to take a coaster wagon on a spin down the Andes. Kathy made an entry in the log, "Queen Charlotte, the lady she's not for crossing now," and we put back to the Landing. In there it was a good day for fishing for black cod, and Kathy did, returning her catches to the water. She says it's the sporting way. I notice she eats fresh-caught fish, however, when I clean them.

On June 20 we tried earlier, at 0500. We filled a thermos with coffee before setting out, knowing that drinking coffee from a cup would be impossible and that the dawn mission wouldn't be possible, either, without coffee. The waves were exuberant again, ten feet, but the sky was blue, and with that to look up at, and take hope, we crossed Kathy's lady, Queen Charlotte. It took us about four and a half hours. Considering that the *Triumph I* can do thirty knots, and that the distance was seventy miles, we spent as much time riding uphill on the water, and losing distance sliding downhill, as we did gaining on that heaving sea. No matter. We did it, and we were proud, and I will not apologize for looking over my shoulder as we came in to Hardy Bay and thumbing my nose at that turbulent witch, Queen Charlotte. Charlotte doesn't sound like a properly queenly name to me now.

We took on gas at Hardy Bay. Our range was three

hundred miles. I like a safety margin that is reasonable, say about twice as much fuel as should be needed for the distance planned to be covered. That is pre–Air Force conduct on my part. The Point of No Return is a challenge to John Wayne, in a romantic script, but we didn't have a scriptwriter to haul us out of the tight spots if we became careless.

We were met at Hardy Bay by the owner of the local fishery, where we regretfully turned down a provisioning of salmon, and then took a heading on Westview. That is reached by way of the Dent Islands and the Yaculta Narrows. Kathy, for the first time, was apprehensive about tricks of seamanship, in that passage. I put on my best Captain Ahab face. We had missed the low slack but the current was loafing, only three knots, and we made the passage neatly. I maintained a What-else? air, despite my surprise that the passage was far more simple than I had expected. The secret of being a successful skipper, I was becoming certain, is to convince the crew that all is well and safe in your hands when the water is standing six feet deep in the wheelhouse. Kathy noted in her log that we did not see any whirlpools, a much-touted local thrill and danger. She also noted that we did "fishtail a little." She will know, now, that the fishtailing was the effect of full-throttle crossing of whirlpools. I had confidence in those twin 55's to get us across those devils that appeared too quickly to be dodged. The sensation, crossing them, was somewhat similar to skidding on icy roads in an automobile and regaining control by steering into the skid. Kind of fun, really. On the *Triumph I*, that is. I will never learn to appreciate a skid in an automobile as entertainment.

We docked at Westview at 1725, a twelve-and-a-half-hour day. We had a motel room there. Kathy washed her hair. The staying power, the strength, of a woman is without limit if she can do her hair at regular intervals.

I telephoned the company people at Seattle. It turned out that there had been worrying done there about us, during the two days we had been out of contact, holed up

waiting to cross Queen Charlotte. I reported the concern
to Kathy. She was falling asleep.

She gave it deep, one-second thought, and said, "Worried? Why? We knew where we were."

We spent the night at the motel and awoke brave again,
at 0600, June 21. We had coffee and orange juice. We
looked at the high, open, and handsome sky. We signed
the guest register of the Powell River Chamber of Commerce. We took on gas, and then we took on the Strait of
Georgia, destination Cape Lazo and nothing but clear
skies and good water to wish us well. We followed Vancou-
ver Island down to French Creek, headed into the waters,
and became humble.

The waves overcame us, threw the port engine out of the
water, swirled us, took command of the boat, had us in a
battle that did not seem fair. We took three waves over the
bow. I will not confess to fear. Terror, yes. Terror is acceptable. Airline pilots have a truism in their trade: Flying
is prorated by the hour, 59 minutes and 30 seconds of
boredom and 30 seconds of sheer terror. They exagger-
ate. It cannot be more than 29 seconds of terror, and that
is 28½ seconds too much. Terror is a constructive element, though. It demands a positive response. There were
moments when the noble *Triumph I,* try as it would, could
not have gone ahead and made it safely without terror
pumping adrenalin, making reason work against its better
judgment, which was to plumb quit. This is terribly dra-
matic in sound and content, but do not sneer until you
have been, man and wife, in waves of that magnitude, in
a twenty-foot boat, feeling awfully sorry for yourselves,
and seeing the lovely, green, secure land a blob on the
horizon, so near and yet so impossibly distant.

So I stood up on the wheel, a position I often took. It is
that of a monkey trying to learn to center a football. The
monkey won't master it. The monkey knows it, and I knew
it. But as I stood over the wheel, my legs spread-eagle,
riding and rolling with the *Triumph,* my head above the
windshield and catching the spray or the waves crashing

over, I felt that at least I was holding my own. I was able
to yell back at nature better from that stance.

And on this day of the triumph of sense over Captains
Courageous, I took three waves over the bow and headed
back for French Creek. I followed a freighter going in. He
had not intended to go there, it was not his port of call, but
when he saw the valiant *Triumph* giving up, that freighter
captain said to himself, "If the waters are too much for
Captain Dimond, they are too much for me." I do appreciate a seagoing captain who appreciates me.

At dock, the freighter captain invited us to supper. We
accepted. At 1930, surly because I was drinking a diet-cola
drink when the sun was over the yardarm, I volunteered to
Kathy that the water had calmed. We could make it to the
next cove for the night. And we did, at darkness, after
having apologized to the freighter captain and explained
to him that we greater vessels did have our obligations to
meet. He took it rather well.

The next two days were easy. We made it into Seattle in
good waters, in good time. We had company business to
do, and after the delays of weather and the demands it had
made on us physically, we did want to arrive in Seattle
looking as proper boaters should, rather than like something dragged in by sharks. It isn't now, wasn't then, easy
for me to come off a boat looking acceptable. I look acceptable to me and to other boaters, but the people at the
dock, freshly arrived from a cocktail party, sometimes
have a "Well, really" look on their faces, and my reaction
is "Well, hell." But that was not the Seattle reception.
Those people know boats, boaters, water; Alaska has
spilled down to them. Or they have spilled up to Alaska.
Whatever way the flow, these united states are a winner.

We had made the Inside Passage. It was nine hundred
miles, give or take another nine hundred going up and
sliding back down those swells. Oceanographers tell me
that the swells we met began building off the coasts of
China. That is a Mao thought I can do without.

"One More, Please"

Kathy and I enjoyed having our pictures in the newspaper, any newspaper. We enjoyed being interviewed for radio and television, live or taped. We were hams with a purpose, propagandizing motors for better boating, but we were supposed to be subtle, to avoid a blatant line of salesmanship. Generally, I succeeded, and so did Kathy.

Meet-the-Press was an easy enough proposition, usually. However it seems to me that we worked harder at it than the interviewers did, and there are several good reasons why that is proper. I will go into the reasons, after making this point: Neither Kathy nor I had two bad moments with the press. We had one, and I will take some skin off him in due time, but over the distance we were well received. I know that it is customary to scald the press and the radio and television people, in conversation among people who have had their pictures in the paper or on the screen. I suppose the first several weeks in heaven are spent adjusting halos and complaining about obituaries. Considering all the griping, it is a marvel to me that the only citizens who do not turn their best profile, smile prettily, and wave their hands at the sight of a camera are embezzlers, wife-beaters, and Mafia executives. I admire the press and have that one exception to prove it.

For the benefit and guidance of any who may be inspired to go boating from Juneau to Key West, and expect to be interviewed along the way, I will go into the matter of press relations now.

On the point of working harder than the interviewers did, the explanation is that we were doing the boating, the newsmen were not. So who should know the news of it?

Obviously, the Dimonds. And who was benefiting by the publicity? The Dimonds, again. And who should have done a little homework and read the press releases in advance of interviewing? Wrong. Not the Dimonds. The reporters. It was amazing how many did not.

So the interviews, more often than not, fell into a routine of how fast the *Triumph I* could go, flat out—35 miles an hour—and the horsepower of the engines—55 each— and the fuel capacity—66 gallons and 250-mile range— and how did we get the assignment? Some of the deeper searchers would ask how the *Triumph* got to Alaska in the first place, and we would tell that rather dull, unromantic tale. It was built in Austin, Texas, and shipped by truck to Seattle. It was outfitted, except for silverware, hunting knife, and glacier ice, at Seattle and went from there to Juneau as deck cargo on a freighter.

The killer whales that escorted us at the outset were a publicity bonus. The Inside Passage of Alaska sounds like just another boat ride to anybody who hasn't done it. We were just two somewhat young people, putt-putting along and proving mainly that we had tough, durable backsides. It would be assumed that anybody could do it if the seat cushions held out. And then, along came those lovely killer whales, and the trip had some adventure, after all, to the dockside navigators with pencils and pads in hand.

To an extent, it is my fault that the romance of the trip wasn't emphasized. For instance, I would prefer to call it a voyage, but since most of it was inland waterways, some prudish element in me comes up with the word "trip," instead. I would prefer to put on airs, but I never know which ones fit me.

So the question is, after speaking for the hundredth time of killer whales, why could I not swing easily into some such patter as, "Yes, killer whales are interesting companions, but did I forget to tell you about the time in the Strait of Georgia when—"?

The time in the Strait of Georgia was about two and a

half hours of terror. One of the other sheer-terror episodes was looking for the French Creek inlet in the strait,
and it also caused the only incident of mutiny aboard the
Triumph.

The waves were running on in walls. I would give the
Triumph all she had going up and haul back on the throttles
coming down, timing it to shove them full-on again and
climb the next wall. I could not stay on that monkey's
merry-go-round any way except seated, and I yelled to
Kathy, "Look for the inlet."

She said, "I can't see it."

"I know you can't, sitting there, stand up and look for
it."

She was holding on to the dash with her left hand, holding on to the seat frame with her right, and she was still
going up and down like a child on a runaway pogo stick.
She looked at me with the disbelief of an Indian princess
who had been led by Chief Strongheart to Lover's Leap
and told, "You first, dear."

Kathy said, "Me stand up? Go to hell."

Goodness. I don't know where she picked up such language. I allowed the lapse in shipboard discipline to go
unpunished. It was the only such infraction, and I could
have built it up nicely in dockside interviews, but I did not.
No doubt a few hundred women interviewers would have
been delighted with it, and so I have only myself to blame
for the standardized reporting that the cruise of the *Triumph I* was one big subsidized honeymoon.

Or I could have varied the report of nonending hospitality by telling about the dock we pulled alongside and
thought quaint and promising of an evening of fun and
jokes. The amusement wasn't so much in the dock itself,
because there was not much of it left. It had been built by
Peter the Great, or some earlier Russian in Alaska, and it
was showing its age, softly settling in the water for a doze.
At the end of it, though, flying splendidly in the strong
wind, was the skull and crossbones. Standing beneath the

pirate flag was Captain Kidd, but I did not recognize him on sight. It took his first sentence to make him known.

"You dock here, it costs ye a buck," he said.

I don't know what my expression was. Facial expression, that is. I didn't say anything. So I guess I was just standing there, over the wheel of the *Triumph*, with my mouth open and looking like a freeloader.

"Don't pay the buck, I shoot ye," Captain Kidd said.

I did not tell that story because it is not typical of Alaska. It is not typical of any other place that we touched, either. I mean, occasionally we had tabs that impressed me as highway robbery transferred to boating, but Captain Kidd was the only armed robber we met, with a threat to shoot and the equipment to do it with, and as an experience, he was worth the dollar he demanded. And got. Somehow, I'm abashed now to be telling on him. May Alaska forgive me. He must be left over from the gold rush.

Or I could have volunteered to tell, when we were well along in the rivers of the continental United States, the quaint customs, and practical customs they are, of Alaskan boaters. If you pull in at night to stay over at a shoreline cabin, it will almost certainly be a vacant cabin. Squirrels and mice do not count. They are the owners, and you stay at their suffrance. These cabins will have pieces of gear in them. Some have cans of gasoline. If you have been careless in your estimate of fuel consumption, you are welcome to the gasoline. The next guy to come along may have overestimated, and will leave his surplus. But as you are free to take something, so must you leave something. Soap or an extra suit of long johns or cans of soup. I do not recall what we left at the cabin we took for a night. Salmon, I suppose.

At first, Kathy was nervous about interviews. We both are gregarious, but she is prettier than I am, and therefore she was apprehensive about the cameras, newspaper or television. They didn't bother me. I haven't a thing to lose to anybody's lens. Neither did I have Kathy's problem of

getting her hair done. That was the coaching done by the
company people. Make frequent stops, or as frequent as
possible at the hairdresser, for Kathy. Otherwise they did
not even tell us to smile, whether we felt like it or not.
Usually, we did.

We were interviewed approximately 200 times on television, 230 times by newspaper reporters, and 170 times on
radio. At first, we were easily impressed by ourselves.
When we would be met at, say, the Marshmallow Center
Marina, by a television news crew, we would stay awake
until the newscast was shown, just for the pleasure of
gawking at ourselves. After about two dozen times
around, we did not look any better, to us, than anything
else on television, so we gave up on the Dimonds. The
most dedicated viewer we had was my sister. The three
networks all have outlets in St. Louis, and when we passed
through there, all three had cameramen and reporters at
the riverfront, welcoming the home-folk travelers. My sister, bless her loyal and ingenious self, lined up three
television sets, side by side, and caught us on the ten
o'clock evening news on all three stations. Lucky for her
we only passed that way once. I do not think she could have
kept up the pace.

In contrast to the How-fast-does-she-go? reporter and
the Where-did-you-spend-last-night? reporter, there were
the Thinkers. They would ask me to compare, or contrast,
the boating in Alaska with the boating in the newspaper's
or radio or television station's home waters. Or they
would ask me to give a guideline for any others planning
to make such a trip, heaven forfend that anyone with so
much money to squander should use it so. They were a
pleasure to talk with, and it occurred to me that there must
be only two requirements for obtaining a job in television
in the outlands: be under thirty and overly pleasant.

The standard question was "How are you able to take off
and do a trip such as this?" and that was a delight to me.
I could get in the plug for the sponsor for free. One of the

best interviews took place in New York City, where we expected nothing less than all-pro abilities. Phyllis Batelle asked me, "What work did you do before this?" and I said, "What's work?" I'd been with the *Triumph I* long enough, by then, to think of myself as the last playboy of the Western world, outboard model, the twin-55-horsepower answer to the jet set. It was a nice fantasy while it lasted.

Miss Batelle was splendid. She kept a straight face when I told her that our regimen was to drink nothing stronger than tomato juice, to think clean thoughts when hung up on sandbars, to go to bed before nine o'clock, and to abstain from tobacco. I lit a cigarette.

Said Miss Batelle with a fine smile, "Buster, you're not a boater, you're a buller."

Then we got down to the serious business of an interview.

For more than a hundred years the most standardized line has been the photographer's "One more, please." There have been some excellent variations, such as the shipboard photographer who asked the Queen of Romania for "one more inch, please," the crude souls among his fellow photographers having just asked her to hike the skirt a trifle more, as she posed on the ship's rail, queenlike.

One of the most demanding of the one-more newspaper photographers worked in our home city, St. Louis. He began his career in the 1920's, when newsmen's cameras used powder for flash power. He was Guy Fawkes, with a camera. He was an even-money choice to blow up any event he covered.

He was not a one-more man because he was incompetent, but because he was a perfectionist. He sought art. Within one summer, he arted right into the Great Beyond the world's championship Siamese cat and the world's championship canary. I don't know how the titles were· won or who in the world bestowed them, but I do know the truth of the grand finish of the cat and the canary. For the first time in their combined annals, cat and canary departed in the same fashion, so far as the cause went: they had their pictures taken by this man.

The cat went first. The cat was housed in the Chase Hotel, which is across from the northeast corner of Forest Park and is favored by visiting celebrities, baseball players, visiting Congressmen and other scoundrels on the lam, and for all I know by local debutantes who are not allowed to watch crime-and-violence television at home. Well, the cat wound up at the Chase, and our photographer arrived in the cat's suite, and since this was the pre-air-conditioned age, the window was open. The cat posed like a champion for a half-dozen shots, but on the one-more seventh, facing that gunpowder flash was too much. The cat went out the open window. The cat, I have neglected to mention, was lording it up in a suite on the ninth floor.

The canary didn't have so far to go. It sat on a perch, in or out of a cage, it doesn't matter. Our hero the photographer, caught up in the close-up technique that was coming out of Hollywood, tried for his one-more shot, strong on the flash, and there went the canary. Fricassee. That was the end of the cameraman's career as a photographer of animals. His newspaper never sends him on such assignments now. He only covers boaters, I believe.

Whenever we encountered a one-more photographer, we appreciated him. It meant that he wanted one more angle, one more to take back to the darkroom to see what he had come up with, and that was good for him in his business and for us in ours. There were late afternoons, pulling up to a dock, when the only "one more" I wanted to hear was from a friendly bartender, but Kathy and I both went along with the picture takers, and it was not phony cooperation with the press. I dreaded much more the quick, confident young man with a budding moustache who said, "Smile, please," and hustled back to the newspaper office with his Polaroid.

Now, about that one bad interview. Or unfair interview. It happened rather well along in the trip and into that southern area of chivalry where in the nineteenth century the works of Sir Walter Scott so influenced young male aristocrats that they could not look at a female over age ten without seeing her as a lady needing saving from a dragon. If the neighborhood was in short supply of dragons that season, they'd save her from a base knight. They would duel, those gentlemen schooled in Sir Walter, over a second peek at an exposed ankle under a hoopskirt. So it was a considerable surprise that after one of the few occasions when we went solo instead of dual on the interview, and Kathy did the honors while I was off on business, the local gentleman of the press wrote a story that left in doubt whether the lady—mine—was for boating or for burning.

I picked up the paper in the morning. I read the story. I put my fist through the first several doors I came across, just testing before going to the newspaper office. Then sweet reason took over. Sweet reason is seldom welcome, but it can make a case. The case this time was that outrage, even a few hot words, would not do the cause of the trip a service, would not much reform the reporter, and above all, would hurt Kathy more. And, since she was still in the room, I decided to return, tell her I had called the sponsor, there was a schedule change, and we had to put on all possible speed to make the next stop several hours in advance. No time to stop for breakfast or to call Aunt Minnie, not even to buy newspapers.

That was how it was done. Not until several months later did I learn that heavy-sleeping Dimond had been preceded to the lobby by his wife. She had picked up a paper, had read the story. She was hurt. Next she was angry. She would not show me the paper, she decided, until the overall success of the trip had made that one lump in some oatmeal-head's outlook unimportant. Accept it or not, any of you marriage counselors who also boat, that is the girl's unselfishness.

On
to the
Wide Missouri

Kathy reorganized as soon as we docked at Seattle. Her preoccupation with Laundromats, she said, wasn't doing our image any good if the clothes we put on the images were forever getting mussed and wrinkled in the *Triumph* storage lockers. Those lockers were grand for housing salmon and canned spaghetti and Kathy's fishhooks, but they were murder on shorts. So she went to town like the free-spending sailor she is and bought a suitcase. Her clothes just fit in it. I asked why she did not buy two suitcases, Hers and His fashion. She looked shocked and said something about the expense. So I will digress and say something about the expense of going from Juneau, Alaska, by boat, to Key West, Florida. Perhaps I will discourage a few from doing it. I'd be discouraged myself, without a large corporate angel behind the boat, picking up the tabs as they fall.

Several times I asked one or another of the company angels the total cost of the trip. They outdid one another, giving vague nonanswers. Ed Hanson broke down and became almost specific, saying that he estimated that it cost $300 a week to keep the Dimonds on the water. For seventeen weeks that would come to $5,100. Of itself that doesn't sound too steep. Most young couples on vacation probably spend close to that per week. The catch is taking off from work for seventeen weeks, no pay coming in, all that money going out.

The original arrangement was for the sponsor to pay all expenses and an additional $1,500 for our services, which is a strange way to label the fun we had. The $1,500 was sufficient to keep the mortgage dry on our house while we were boating. I'd have gone in hock to pay the $1,500, or settle for all-expenses-and-even, but I had the good sense to keep that generous notion to myself during the negotiations.

We were given a cash advance of $400, and were to use our own credit cards along the way, submitting an expense account at the end of each week. The only exception was in gasoline. Cities Service—I know the name was changed to Citgo, but it was done without my customer approval—picked up the gas and oil bills. The Cities Service people were very protective. Before we left Juneau, we were told that if we ran out of gas, wherever we were, whatever the time of night or the rage of nature, to pick up a phone or send up a flare, and good old Cities Service would dispatch a rescue truck, tanker, or carrier pigeon toting gas drums. Immediately. Well we did run out of gas once, thirty yards from shore, owing to my bullheaded assertion of captain's judgment over Kathy's. We didn't have to send for Cities Service. An amiable reformed pirate, retired to the marina business, rescued me. Not "rescued *us*" in this instance, because Kathy knew she had been right all along and didn't need rescuing. I told her, as the boat rocked with her laughter, that I had almost been right in estimating the fuel-and-distance propositon. Missing by thirty yards from the destination may be a long way short of the mark if you're a quarterback trying to make it across a goal line, but how many quarterbacks do, by outboard?

The lady herself, meaning the *Triumph I*, could be had for about $5,000, but that does not include the cost of some of the sophisticated gear we had, such as radios and compasses. The engines would come to another $2,000. Then there is that other great expense to tourists everywhere, picture taking. We tried to get Eastman Kodak to provide us the film, but the company's reply to that was, in effect, "Why should we? You will be using our film anyway." Buying it, they meant, and they were correct, to the extent of sixty-seven rolls of color film shot on my Minolta—my own, literally, no commercial hidden there—

at thirty-six exposures to the roll. A telephoto lens was contributed by the company early on in the trip. That was an addition I should have been smart enough to figure out for myself, before we left Juneau.

Anyway, my guess is that the nonboating gear in the *Triumph,* from that tree saw, which I assume is still somewhere at the bottom of the storage locker, to the telephoto lens and the dime-store silverware Kathy bought, had a retail value of about $2,000.

Altogether that comes to $14,000, and I have not included the cost of some 3,300 gallons of gasoline or the cost of putting the Dimonds in your boat. Maybe you'd rather leave us on shore, and if so I don't blame you. It's a grand adventure and an expensive one, but Kathy summed up one large aspect of it when she said, "I don't think we've done anything spectacular, of ourselves. I think the trip is much more a compliment to the equipment we've had than it is to us."

Summing it up, I'd say that such a trip would be feasible for a young couple if they came from the right branch of the Rockefeller family. There is a poor branch, you know. And unless the boat you use is bunk-equipped, as ours was, lodging will be an expense. When we spent the night in motels, marinas, or yacht clubs, or as guests on cabin cruisers, it was mainly for the availability of a shower.

By way of money, I will get the trip back on the water, resuming where I left off, in Seattle. Before we left Seattle on June 24, I made two telephone calls. I came to regard telephones as the most evil necessity of the trip. After we departed Juneau, we were met by men from the sponsoring company's main office only at St. Louis, Milwaukee—no avoiding them, there—New York, and Jensen Beach, Florida. It was their policy to leave us alone, independent, to prove that any man and wife can go boating eight thousand miles and not need to be held by the hand. Modern equipment can do that reassuring job. But they did want to know we were alive and well and where we intended to be the next day. It was not as much of an annoyance as

having to call home after a high-school dance and ask for
an hour's extension on the family curfew. The first telephone call I made in Seattle was not to the company, however, but to a cousin in St. Louis, my lawyer.

I asked him, "Did you get the expense check yet from
the company?"

"No, I assumed you hadn't turned in the expense accounts, and that's what is holding it up."

I had turned in the expense accounts. And that is when
I made an extra call, to Milwaukee. The matter turned out
to be simple enough. A secretary in Ed Hanson's office
had the tabs all on hand, neatly filed, and she was patiently
waiting for us to get to New York so she could total the
bundle. She thought that the $400 advance was to last us
for the entire trip. If that girl budgets herself as closely as
she had it in mind to budget us, she should buy up Standard Oil in a few more years.

Solvent again, we headed for Olympia, Washington,
where we would pull the boat and make the first of our two
portages, a short one to Kelso, Washington. That is a
splendid boat ride, Seattle to Olympia, because it is by way
of Tacoma and its resident marvel, Mount Rainier. It was
putting on a special show that day, its base hidden in a
haze, so that the peak seemed detached, an immense and
independent production floating by its snow-topped self
in a world of its own.

We lost our status as an Alaskan fish boat at Olympia.
Before we pulled the boat from the water, to put it on a
trailer for the overland to Kelso, we were to give the governor of Washington the gift of fish from the governor of
Alaska, but Governor Evans of Washington couldn't make
it to pick up his fish. He sent an aide to accept it for him,
and the aide seemed delighted with his task. Maybe I
should have asked for a receipt. He might not have been
so delighted if the original governor-to-governor gift, as
proposed by our guardian Bill Pearsall, had come off.

"Thirty pounds of fish is a fine gift, a sound gift, a
thoughtful gift," said Pearsall. "Any governor would be

pleased to have it around the mansion, but let us accept
the basic fact of fish: they won't last long if they are kept
out where the governor's friends can admire them, as a
gift should be admired, so why not send the governor
something Alaskan that will keep, and what's more will
grow on him, not that the fish wouldn't, you understand,
but something that has a little more personality than a cold
salmon."

"Such as what, Bill?"

"Why, an Alaskan wolfhound pup," said Pearsall. "Now,
there is a gift that will be a constant reminder to one
governor of another every time he scratches it behind the
ears. Could he do that with the fish?"

Ed Hanson nodded. I looked at Kathy. These two plu-
perfect geniuses were serious about shipping us out with
a pup. Then Hanson's expression changed to sorrow, the
bereavement of a man who has seen a grand scheme crash
into the facts of life and shatter, leaving only beautiful but
worthless fragments of the what-might-have-been.

"Won't work, Bill," said Hanson.

"Won't work? Why those are the workingest dogs you
ever—"

"No, Bill, I mean it won't work on the boat. Where are
Kathy and Bill going to walk the pup when they're at sea?"

Before Bill could figure out pontoon booties for the
pup, we finished our martinis and said it was time for
dinner, and so far as we know, that is why the governor of
Washington does not have an Alaskan wolfhound.

The trailer haul to Kelso was 59 miles. Only then, and
on the 400-mile portage from Lewiston, Idaho, to Fort
Benton, Montana, did I feel foolish. There was the *Triumph
I*, going down a highway on a trailer for the whole, wide
skeptical world to see and read the proud legend on her
sides, "Juneau, Alaska, to New York City." I could hear
some tourist saying later, when our tip-to-tip tour of the
United States by boat was mentioned to him, "Those fak-
ers? Sure, I saw them and their boat, doing sixty miles an
hour it was, on a trailer. Where? Oh, I don't rightly

remember, somewhere about the Mojave Desert, I think."

We put back in on the Cowlitz River at Kelso, and took a shortcut through the Multnomah Channel, but still arrived in Portland thirty minutes late for a scheduled reception. It was, I'd been told on the ever-hot line to Milwaukee, the first really big reception that had been scheduled for us, with boat and engine dealers from miles around assembled to point proud fingers at what their products were accomplishing. In coming in to Portland, my first thought was "My, my, what big ships they have here." It's an awesome sight to a country-river boy when he finds himself mixing, in an outboard, with his betters towering above him. My second thought, a few minutes later, was that all those proud dealers would be pointing at the splinters of their products in a second or two because some idiot helmsman had changed course in a large boat and showed every intention of running us down.

I yelled, "My God, Kathy, I've got the right of way, but this damn fool's trying to run us off the river."

"Language, language," she said. "It's the Portland fireboat and they're glad to see you and are welcoming you to town," and with that the fireboat went into its act. I had never seen a fireboat before, and neither had Kathy, and what right does a woman have to be so often correct with feminine guesses? It is the only disadvantage to man-and-wife boating. Wives should be required by law to leave the feminine intuition on shore and boat the hard way, without it, the way men do.

We did our commercial duty at Portland, and although we were to do that several hundred more times along the way, we decided that one man among the Portland dealers had already won our Croix de Salesmanship. We did not expect to meet another who would make as much racket over the opportunity, and we didn't. He had a bullhorn, and he was trumpeting a sales pitch to half of Portland: "The water's beautiful, folks, just beautiful, now's the time to buy a boat and come on out and run with the Dimonds."

We pressed on, to Camas, Washington, before any of

The *Triumph* out for her first portage, the 400 miles from Olympia, Washington, to Kelso, Washington.

The Portland, Oregon, fireboat, replete with dignitaries out to meet us.

his customers could hitch on with us. I knew we had two rough days ahead of us on the Columbia River, and I wanted to get it over with. I had been told that the Columbia thinks it is an ocean and puts on an open-sea act quite often, just to reassure itself that it is all that big and tough.

The Columbia tried especially hard to impress us. The natives along the way denied that, of course. They swore on their holiest of holies, the guidebooks, that the Columbia was on its good behavior. They said we should have been on it last week. I don't know why we should have been on it last week, I said to myself at the time, and at the end of two days and 160 miles I could not figure out why we should have been on it any one minute, much less any one week. Its roughness truly did come up to some oceanic standards, and I do not approve of rivers that carry on so.

I am grousing, of course, for the exercise of it, partly. It also relieves the pace of reporting a pleasure trip that hummed along nicely, from one pleasure to the next. The ordeal began easily enough, and impressively, with locking through at the Bonneville Dam. That was our first locking through. Over the distance we would do it ninety-two times.

We went up forty-seven feet and it was easy handling, with not too much competition from the wind. We thought that was an impressive rise, forty-seven feet, and were proud of ourselves, but the lockmaster was true to the Columbia code. Said it was nothing, we should have been there last week, or some one of those much-famed previous weeks, when the river was low and locking through was a matter of a sixty-foot rise.

The day was cloudless, the sun was at tanning warmth without any malicious intent to burn, the scenery was a threat to navigation because a man would prefer watching it to watching where he was driving a boat, and the water was miserable. Waves were as high as the boat. Since the waves could not quite make it over the bow, they did the

vengeful, natural thing for waves to do, and pounded away
at the tailbones of the *Triumph* and her crew. We stopped
for the night at the Dalles, and the next morning at 0630
Kathy was cheerful and eager for more Columbia. That did
not surprise me. The motel at the Dalles started off her day
with coffee and rolls. Kathy's log reads like a travelogue
from restaurant to restaurant by boat. Start that girl's day
off with fine pastry and promise her lobster or steak at the
end of the boating day, and she will take on the Columbia
in an inner tube.

At the boat basin, I made some ungracious remarks
about the wind. A man working there came in, right on
cue. He said the winds weren't much of anything now,
hardly enough to ruffle the feathers on a chicken. I should
have been there a couple of hours ago, he said. Better yet,
I should have been at his house, couple of hours after
midnight. The wind came up then and blew the screens off
his house.

We put through the Dalles Dam, and then the Columbia
bade us its fondest farewell. The waves had been practicing and were able to make it across the bow, and they were
not one-of-a-kind waves, except in orneriness. Every so
often a cross-wave would appear, fretful that we might
become bored with its straight-on cousins, and would belt
us a good one and swing the *Triumph* about. When we
came to the pull-out point, we met two other groups in
boats, cabin cruisers. They were the only other boaters we
had seen. They had planned a cruise to Portland, but both
skippers said the Columbia was too much for them this
week. Not last week, praise be, but this week. They were
taking their boats out of the water.

We stood on land or leaned into the wind and stood as
best we could, and looked at the sea gulls parked overhead. Their wings were going, but the birds headed into
the wind were not going anywhere. They held their own,
and that was all. Forward progress was impossible. It was
the day's only bonus. I have not felt kindly toward sea gulls

Columbia River whitecaps at Celilo Falls, Oregon.

At Celilo Falls a windy day means winds of 50 to 60 miles an hour.

since the night one dropped a fish head in the stern of the *Triumph.* It proved to be a valuable relic of a fish head, something that had been in the gull's family for years and was so much the envy of the neighbors that they swooned whenever the proud owner came downwind of them. We swooned too.

Kathy was enchanted by the Columbia. She said she did not want to leave it, but that it was nice to know that it would keep, as a challenge, that it would always be there. Well, if it moves anywhere else, I do not intend to go looking for it. Those several days comprised one of the few tedious runs, a span that was not a pleasure but a burden. I don't know. If Kathy feels that way about the Columbia and is happy that it is going to stay put and wants to come back to it as a challenge, perhaps I was having forty-eight hours of grumpiness. Any river hemmed in by such scenery can't be all bad.

We broke up the portage to Fort Benton by putting the boat into the water at Coeur d'Alene, just for the boating hell of it. Kathy did not boat with me there. I got on the water by myself, and looked about, and felt like an ingrate to Kathy, God, water, the Columbia, and the sponsors, and came back to the dock a soothed, and boating, man again.

When we arrived at Fort Benton and parked the *Triumph,* Kathy went scouting. For a Laundromat, of course. A police officer came to the truck and asked who owned the boat. I said I did. It beat telling a policeman it wasn't my boat, really, but that I knew the people who owned it and was looking after it for them until it got to New York. Never strain the credulity and patience of the law, I always say.

"Okay, son, but you got to get it out of here. You can't park a boat on the main drag in Fort Benton."

He was a sensible man. So we put the boat in the fabled wide Missouri. What the fable leaves out is its depth, up there in Montana. Not enough depth to bother mentioning, the fable-makers agree.

"Liars of the Old West"

The romance of steamboating is the exclusive property of the Mississippi, mostly because Mark Twain said that is how it had to be assigned. There was steamboat traffic on the Missouri, too, however, and considering the size of the boats and the inability of the river to make up its mind whether to be two miles wide and two inches deep, in Montana especially, or to rearrange its dimensions into something more reasonable, it is a marvel that the traffic was as heavy as it became in the 1860's. Or perhaps it is just a tribute to that great driving force, human cussed- ness. A man can look at the Missouri at Fort Benton and know full well it is no place for a steamboat. So the man is obliged to bring a steamboat there.

A short history of the Missouri that I read, while racked up on one midstream mudshelf or another, stated that the first steamboat arrived at Fort Benton in 1859. The last steamboat freight was unloaded at Fort Benton in 1888. The peak steamboat year in Fort Benton was 1867, when thirty-seven boats managed to reach there, and it required some management because some of those steamboats carried four hundred passengers. Those were large steamboats.

Charles M. Russell, the cowboy artist, was a St. Louisan who found his career in Montana. He arrived there too late for the last steamboat and had to be content with cowboys, Indians, and horses in his art, but he did appreciate good river stories. In his book, *Trails Plowed Under,* Russell wrote a chapter headed, "Some Liars of the Old West." It is a fine book, and I think it is a tribute to the inspirational powers of the Missouri River that Russell would include a

66

story about it in what was basically a tribute to high, wide, and handsome cowboy liars.

Russell wrote, "The upper Missouri River steamboats, they used to say, would run on a light dew, an' certainly they used to get by where there was mighty little water. X. Beidler an' his friend, Major Reed, are traveling by boat to Fort Benton. One night they drink more than they should. X. is awakened in the morning by the cries of Reed. On entering his stateroom, X. finds Reed begging for water, as he's dying of thirst.

"X. steps to the bedside, and taking his friend's hand, says, 'I'm sorry, Major, I can't do anything for you. That damned pilot got drunk, too, last night, and we're eight miles up a dry coulee.' "

More than 80 percent of the precious metals mined in Montana in the steamboating era went from the territory to the states by steamboat. They were thinkers, those boatmen. They would load the boats so that the prow was one foot deeper in the water than the aft end. When the boat got hung up, the crewmen would shift the cargo weight to the rear, springing the front end loose. They had special decor on those boats, too. The pilot houses were sheathed in boiler iron, the better to bounce off the bullets fired at them by Indians. It was our misfortune to come along one hundred years too late for the excitement.

When we put into the water at Fort Benton, the morning of July 1, we waited at the ramp for a descendant of the keelboat men to bring up to land his handcrafted work of art. It was a forty-foot johnboat. He had built it in two sections. He was completing a cruise, pleasure cruise, he called it, from Fort Benton to Fort Peck, some 330 miles distant, and return. The Fort Peck Lake, a reservoir formed by the Fort Peck Dam at the eastern head of the Missouri River basin in Montana, is 16 miles wide at one point, and when it has reached full growth the lake will be 180 miles long. It is the loneliest stretch we encountered on the trip. It is no place to run out of gas. The johnboat

An old steamboat wreck, flattened by a century, lies stripped and
sun-bleached beside the Missouri River in Montana.

builder knew that. His fuel dump on board consisted of thirty 5-gallon gas cans.

Following my conviction that no boatman can have too many charts, I had been chart hunting in Fort Benton. The latest I could find was a chart dated, I believe, 1888. It must have been left behind by the last steamboat captain when he headed for home on foot. I asked the johnboat skipper if he had anything later than that, and he said he certainly did, the very latest charts published on the first stretch of the Missouri that we would be traveling. No, he would not think of allowing us to pay for them. They were his gift to us, his expression of God-speed, and he advised us to hang on to them. We could pass them on to our children if ever they made the trip. He was confident the charts he was giving us would still be, twenty-five years or more from now, the most modern available for that portion of the river. His charts were from 1893. Having gained five years in the modernity of our charts, we set out more confidently.

There were others putting out on the Missouri, a group that had come from Albuquerque because they had heard of the magnificent high-lonesome quality of the country the river cuts through. They were the most diversified group of boaters we met. They had in their fleet a kayak, a canoe, and a rubber life-raft. They were also knowledge-able. They had appointed a quartermaster officer to go into town and avail himself of all bug repellent available. That amounted to the few aerosol bombs we had left on the store shelves.

Wilderness closed in, and the privacy of it all led Kathy to expose her back in a two-piece bathing suit. The biggest part of the top, I've complained to her at swimming pools, is the bow tie at the back, and there's not much to that bow. She sat in the Montana sun, happy with the tan she was getting, and for several of the painful days thereafter she had a signature-souvenir of the day, the perfect outline of the bow, pale against the sunburn. It was the only case of aching sunburn on the trip, a statistic that I present smugly because carelessly overdoing the sunbathing is one of the perils of boating.

We mushed along on one engine, playing the game the river's shallow way. Occasionally we were grounded, but by shutting down the engine, I could pole us off, get out and push us off, or just sit and wait for the Missouri to release us in its own good time. It is not countryside to be hurried through, anyway, especially in the Stone Walls region. There are landmarks that were named by the early explorers and the steamboat captains: Hay Stack Butte, Castle Rock, Citadel Rock, Cathedral Rock, Steamboat Rock, Castle Bluff. They were not unimaginative men, those early christeners of rock formations. The names they gave match the shapes, at least as well as do the names I give cloud formations when I'm up in an airplane, playing poet where no one can catch me at it.

That country has everything except crowds. At Fort Benton someone told me to look closely when we passed Hole in the Wall, that we would see Chief Cochise in there, but we should not expect him to wave and say howdy. He is no more genial now, apparently, than he was in his prime against the Seventh Cavalry, but my informant said the sight of him would be kind of cheerful after seeing nothing except elk and cows. Cochise wasn't home when we went by Hole in the Wall, and I think I know the business that had called him out. A mile or so down the river from his place, we saw a man and a horse, high on a cliff, in outline against the sky.

The man was lifting something that required strength to budge, slowly straightening his back, raising his arms to give distance to the throw he was about to make. Then the dark form of whatever he was pitching over that high rocky bluff was out of our sight, and so, as abruptly, were the man and his horse. Kathy says what we saw was a cowboy getting rid of a bad batch of biscuits. I know better. We saw Cochise, adding another scalp, getting rid of the excess baggage of his trophy. A cowman later told me it was probably an Indian, all right, but an up-to-date one on the reservation, and following his wife's instructions to get rid of the week's trash. Okay, Kathy's happy with her biscuit theory, the cowman's happy with his explanation that it's a henpecked Indian, and I'm happier than both of them put together. I've got Cochise.

When under way, en route to the reservoir, the only sounds we heard other than "Bill, I think we're stuck again" and "Yes, dear" were the protest uproars of the cattle and the elk. It took us well into the second day to determine the basis of their complaints: All the bulls were on one side of the Missouri River and the cows on the opposite side, and they thought the government should do something about it. That note of frustrated romance reminded me, when we passed the mouth of the Judith River, of a touching story about Captain Clark of the Lewis and Clark partnership.

Clark actually organized that expedition in Virginia, where he launched it, in the important sense that he received funds sneaked out the back door of the Treasury by Thomas Jefferson. One fine Sunday, out for an afternoon of socializing, Clark paused at a house whose membership included a beautiful daughter. He was smitten.

Dissolve scene: Captain Clark is now up the Missouri, without a map, free to make his own map and give names as he goes. The party passes this fine little stream. Clark, that belle of Virginia as clear in his memory as are the waters of the unnamed little river, says, "I dub thee the Judith River," or whatever formula it is explorers use for formal naming of rivers and such.

Two years later, back in Virginia, he returned to the home of the belle. She had been about fifteen that first and only other day he had seen her. At the first opportunity, he informs her of the little thing he has done for her. Named a river after her. Yes, ma'am, two thousand miles away there is your very own namesake, the Judith River.

The turrets of Citadel Rock loom over us as we cruise the upper Missouri.

And she blushed shyly and told him, nice try, close but no cigar. Her name was Julia.

He never got back Montana-way to correct it, but he did get her name straight. She got his, too. She married him.

It had been arranged, before we left Fort Benton, that we would be met at Robinson Bridge by Jim Chandler, the Army Corps of Engineers biologist for the Fort Peck Dam area. The Robinson Bridge designation as a meeting place sounded to us like nothing more than a convenience, and the only one of its kind in that whole long stretch from Fort Benton to the dam. That bridge is more than a convenience, it is a social center for that vast land. Chandler set the tone for the hospitality we would meet there.

Our rendezvous time had been 1445, and we were there on time. Chandler had been there since noon, in case we were early, which he doubted. He had brought his tent and other camping gear in his truck, in case he had to overnight at the bridge if we were delayed, which he expected. He did not seem to consider his coverage of either eventuality as going out of his way for two strangers. Just the Montana way, nothing unusual about it.

He had brought three 5-gallon gas cans, all he had available. Topping up the *Triumph* would require several trips to the settlement near the bridge. The settlement was one gas pump, attached to a bar and café. The only thing in sight around it, horizon to horizon, was Montana landscape. I went into the bar and had a beer with Chandler and listened to the men talking. They were having a beer before getting into whichever pickup truck they'd hitched outside and driving to whatever small spot in that large landscape was home to them. They were friendly men, and it occurred to me that they were at an oasis, in that bar, in a valid sense of the word.

Robinson Bridge was a camping site because of the fishing and the nearby oasis. They were great for moseying over, those Montana campers and fishermen. One moseyed over with fresh-caught catfish, and another with homemade cookies. We turned in at dusk, about 2230, and as I took a last look at the shore, from the berth on the *Triumph,* I noticed a considerable number of car lights, a crowd by local standards. Jim had told me it would happen, and it is good for our humility that he had. Those people hadn't driven in from the nowhere to see us, the intrepid boaters. They had simply decided to put the family in the car, this fine summer night, and drive for a look at the biggest sight available in that land, the Robinson Bridge.

At 0630 we were preparing to get under way. That should have required me to get in the water and shove us away from the bank, but that could not be allowed for the stranger-visitors to the Robinson Bridge. People had roused themselves at the first sound of our stirring about, and they insisted that we stay aboard while they waded in to give us their parting gift—a dry-shod start of the day for me.

We got out into the current, and I eased back and decided that there are more Robinson Bridge people in this world than I had ever had the time or the chance to suspect when I was living in a world of folding doors. I said to Kathy, "Tell me, as one river rat to another, casting up on one mudbank or another and taking social potluck, what do you think of people?"

She grinned. "They're great."

And Down the Line: St. Louis

We made the run from the social center of central Montana, the Robinson Bridge, to the Fort Peck Dam, on the Fourth of July, and a bang-up celebration of a run it was. Ten miles down from the bridge we were into the lake. For several miles it was boating on a forest top. The lake hasn't filled yet, and at that still-shallow end of it the timber wasn't removed before the water began moving in. Once past that, into the main body of water, it was the richest day of being spoiled by easy boating, fast mile-covering boating, that we had had.

After Fort Peck Dam, we were back on the familiar Missouri River, plowing up Montana with our props, checking the trusty 1893 charts, and agreeing that the Missouri is a fairly stable river—just skims along the surface from one century to the next. It was in that stretch, creeping up on the North Dakota line, that we rounded a bend and came upon a bridge under construction. That bridge would come as a surprise to the men who did our charts. It did to me, and it was the author of the only accident we had with the *Triumph*.

The pilings for the bridge had been poured, and the works had a ramp about four feet high running across them. I took down the antenna, slowed almost to a halt, and chose what seemed the widest opening between the piers. We could clear the ramp, but not by much, and I eased into the thing. Easy always does it in those waters if you have any feeling for your boat's undersides in uncertain situations. I mean, easy almost always does it. Easy didn't do it this time, because there was sufficient water at the pilings to sponsor a sudden crosscurrent, and it carried Captain Cautious smack into the piling, broadside, on my side of the *Triumph.* The collision rattled my teeth, ripped the gunwale on my side, put a permanent bend in the rub rail, and dumped my pride so low I couldn't have gotten to it with the U.S.S. *Missouri*'s bilge pumps, but it did not damage the Glastron toughness of the hull. I tried to calculate the force at work, the 3,500-pound load of the *Triumph* hitting the piling at eight miles an hour. I gave up for fear I'd arrive at an answer. I had answer enough in the splinters from the piling, splinters that had been driven about an inch into the boat.

In such moments I say the wrong thing. I don't have to think about it. The shabby comment has been there all my life, just waiting for the moment of its release. I am fully confident it will realize its moment and spring forth.

Looking at my side of the boat, I said, "It looks like an airline stewardess I used to date."

Before we got into more traveled waters, I was able to get a cosmetics job done on the gunwale, but there remained for the rest of the trip that bend in the rub rail. Looking at it every once in a while, when feeling successful and salty, became a good safety procedure for me. Instant desalinization of the Dimond ego.

Through North and South Dakota, the Missouri is almost entirely dams and reservoirs. Some of the lakes are adolescents, and it was the familiar routine of picking our way over treetops, barn roofs, and fence posts. The largest body of water in North Dakota is Lake Sakakawea (Garrison Reservoir). I never had cause, previously, to wonder how much water there is in North Dakota. If I had, I'd have been shy by about 210 miles in length, and at one point, 52 miles in width, because I didn't know about Lake Sakakawea. I was pleased to make its acquaintance in its main body, because it permitted wide-open throttles. I was afraid, after those stretches of the Missouri, that the engines might have forgotten what that was. They hadn't.

In South Dakota, reading from the top down, there are

the waters of the Oahe Reservoir, Lake Sharpe, and Lake Francis Case. It is a border-to-border string and I worried about keeping the gas supply safely up. I need not have worried. Western hospitality was still in effect. At one bankside stop, a farmer was indignant when I tried to pay him for the gas. At another, near Sutton's Bay, the gas again was a gift, but the giver tried to fend off protests or, worse yet, gratitude, by saying, "Pay me? Why? Hell, I stole it."

Then we met Fred McQuistion, proprietor and pundit of Pike Haven Resort. If you're ever out that way in an automobile, you'll have no trouble finding Pike Haven. It is twenty-six miles west of Onida, South Dakota. If you are alarmed about being able to find Onida, do not be. It is unfounded alarm. Just get into the south end of South Dakota and roll down the window. Soon enough you will hear Fred, and homing on his voice, you will roll right through Onida and find yourself, twenty-six miles west-ward, at Pike Haven.

We came to Fred's place low on gasoline. Kathy went to his office to inquire about gasoline while I stayed at the *Triumph* to look at the props and debate changing them. I won the debate. No change needed. Kathy, meanwhile, wasn't certain what she was winning or losing.

"Gasoline?" said McQuistion. "Certainly, little lady, just a little old five miles down the road, and I got these dandy gasoline drums here. Tell you what we'll do, you just roll them down the road to the station and I'll get the funnel here and put it in the Scout, and I'll be there waiting for you, have everything set up at the station by the time you get there."

Fred looks like a cowboy, dresses like a cowboy, talks like a cowboy. Kathy could appreciate that. She hasn't been much exposed, however, in girls' schools and other roughhouse centers to the delicacy of cowboy humor. By the time I came into McQuistion's office, I think he had about convinced her we should trade in the *Triumph* on two pack mules he had out back and finish the trip the comfortable, Western way.

After a few minutes, McQuistion allowed that fun's fun, but we should be getting the gas. He put the big cans in the back of the Scout, a vehicle that I suspect is a Jeep with hyperthyroid, and invited me to ride with him. I saw what had the appearance of a road leading out of his place. It looked like an acceptable road to me. Fred ignored it. He headed for a cliff. At the top of it, he popped the clutch and took us into space, as close as I have ever been to a carrier-deck takeoff.

We landed right side up. The McQuistions of this world always do. Shortcut, he explained. Roads are all right for tourists. Tourists should be pampered, but what is the value of being a native if you don't know the shortcuts? When we returned with the gas, he stopped while unloading it and frowned. He had forgotten something at the gas station. He turned to his son and told him to get in the Scout and go to the station for him. Fred's son didn't take the cliff route. He went the sedate path, down the road, as any eight-year-old driver should. When the boy is ten, Fred may give him cliff-jumping privileges with the Scout, as a birthday present.

McQuistion was our last touch of the Wild West, real or simulated. I do not mean that there is anything made-up about Fred. He is real enough, and if I could be Fred I wouldn't trade his life for all the folding doors that are now or ever will be. Kathy wouldn't like it, though. Not enough Laundromats around.

The waters in that vertical string of lakes and reservoirs in South Dakota were sunswept, windswept, and shallow. Wind and shallow water can be a bad combination. In New Orleans, when high winds make Lake Pontchartrain impossible, and the boys are sitting inside hoisting one and saying they've seen it worse, one of them is duty-bound to remember the day he was caught out there, and the wind just scooped up the water on that shallow old lake, not two

hundred yards ahead of him, and for a second there he saw
the lake bed, as dry as any restaging of the parting of the
Red Sea a man could hope to see.

We were not treated to that, trying to get in to Fort Peck,
but it was bad enough for Kathy to put on a life jacket, and
I gave in to her fears and took the shelter of an inlet.
Another night of canned spaghetti. However, I did have
the overhead patched to the point now that we could live
with it. The overhead got to be a hobby, really, a comfort,
something to make me feel necessary on the boat. Everything else worked so well that it was nice to feel needed.
I also began to feel superior. There is not much boating
in the Dakotas, considering the expanse of water. At one
stop a native was having trouble. He could not start his
engine.

His wife sat forward, saying all the wifely things that help
start engines, such as, "I told you we needed a washer and
drier more 'n we did this thing," and, "So this is boating,
broiling in the sun."

I volunteered to take a look at his engine, and he agreed.
It was one way to silence his wife. She was a decent sort.
She didn't chew on him when company dropped in. So I
looked at the engine and tried not to grin and hunched
over it in an attempt to conceal from him what I was doing.
I connected his gas line. If he hadn't had those distractions
from up forward, he surely would have seen it for himself.
As it was, he saw it when I made the connection. He turned
red.

His wife said, "See, if you'd learn something about it
before you went off on the fool things." He thanked me,
but I don't think his heart was in it. Kathy was amused, but
she understood the moral of it. If someone is in trouble,
I feel obliged to offer help, and if they don't want it they
have the option to tell me so in language of their own
choice. It's fair enough. Maybe they'll give me the same
opening someday.

At Fort Randall, the fifth of six dams we had to go

around, pull the boat out on one side and dump it in on the other and listen to the trailer crew's cussing wonderment at how a small boat could be so heavy, I laid in a fresh and valuable new stock of humility. The Army Corps of Engineers had us met by a guide, Milo Brown. The next passage, below Fort Randall, was tricky, but Milo, it was said, was right good at reading the water there.

Read it? He could interpret it in Chinese or Sanskrit. If that was too difficult for the pupil to follow, Milo would put it into something easy, like Choctaw. He managed to pound a few of the basics into me, such as reading deep water in ripples and shallow in glassy-flat water, studying floating leaves for movements, and suspecting at cutbanks that the current followed the outside of the bend, close to the channel. That is kindergarten, I know, to experienced rivermen. Since I don't expect to make it to the first grade, much less to Milo's cum-laude ranking, I was grateful for the primer learning he was able to give me during a short run.

Twenty-one miles above Sioux City we met a navigational marker. It was like stepping out of the woods and finding yourself at Times Square with a Boy Scout waiting to help you across the street.

"Kathy, we're home free," I said. "No more guessing the channels, it's all idiot's work now."

I had done it again, sold that river short. We'd no sooner sighted that first buoy and headed for it, the better to get a close loving look at it, than it went under the water. The river was high and the current was sucking it under. The cans—black and white buoys—and the nuns—the red ones —are saviors of careless boaters when the buoys are sitting pretty. Submerged, as that one became, they can be a trap. A buoy is three feet in diameter, five feet high, and weighs seven hundred pounds. The cable holding it is strong in proportion to its captive. Hit one, and you have lost a boat, likely as not. A couple in Sioux City preferred to tell us about a couple in a runabout that dodged the buoy then had their boat sliced in half by the cable. They solemnly agreed there was not a section of the Missouri, or the Mississippi, either, that had more buoys so talented in slicing boats in half. It is one of the prides of boaters that whatever stretch of the river or ocean or millpond is home to them has the most cunning challenges to skill known to man. If thinking so adds to their fun, why argue?

Sioux City is the terminus of the barges. The upstream dams would get in the way of a barge, of course, but I think it's equally reasonable to assume the barges halt at Sioux City and dare poke no farther upstream because that fine old steamboat-pilot talent for going eight miles up a dry coulee is a vanished art. In addition to being the terminus of the barges, the river waters at Sioux City were also the beginnings of water pollution. Logs, outhouses, and barn doors in a river are not pollution. A river is a natural collector, and goes out of its way and over its banks to get things it wants to take along with it, but the dregs that man throws into it, which the river didn't ask for and doesn't want, are an insult to the river. And the rivers and the lakes, we noticed, are beginning to get their revenge by going along with man's dirty games. Rivers and lakes can't lick us, so they will join us in our sloppiness, and it will serve us right in another twenty years if in our nice boats we're all fishing in oil slicks. Or detergent pools. End of sermon.

We were due in St. Louis July 23. We would have family reunions, meetings with our sponsor, and radio and newspaper interviews for the local couple that would be at about the halfway point of making good on what still stood as a Juneau-to-New York motorboat trip. If we had a minute's time out from all that, we would also lift a glass to each other and say, "Happy wedding anniversary." (We took the time out.)

The homecoming began as soon as we were in the state of Missouri's part of the Missouri. At St. Joe the Coast Guard came out to meet us. The guardsmen were wearing life jackets. We felt guilty. We always kept the life jackets at hand, but if we had been copy-book-perfect boaters on the trip we would have had them on at all times. And would have died of heat prostration somewhere on the Missouri River. Waving at the Coast Guardsmen and their nice orange jackets, Kathy laughed. I asked what was funny.

"The Coast Guard. It changes style."

"Looks like the same Coast Guard style we've seen everywhere else to me."

"No, Bill, it's different because they're the first we've seen wearing life jackets. The others didn't, even in Alaska."

It was an easy three days down the Missouri from Kansas City, to arrive in St. Louis on the twenty-third. There were a few diversions. At Kansas City we docked for an interview. I had thought of some excellent lines to throw off about boating the upper Missouri. Sort of the Lewis and Clark expedition, as told by Noel Coward. Then a pile driver started up, stage center. We were outshouting that when a mile-long freight train went by, stage left. I didn't see that interview on television, but I am proud of it. Has the best sound effects in the history of boating.

Traffic on the river increased in pleasure boats, and more noticeably in barge tows, from Kansas City. Kathy had never crossed the wake of a barge before, and she did not approve of the commotion it causes in a boat such as the *Triumph.* I asked her to think of a way around it. In more than three hundred miles, she couldn't. The girl does have her limitations. The limitations do not include a lack of affability, the ability to get along with the sort of people I would rather meet off the water than on it. Off the water, I could walk away from them. On the water, we met people on the Missouri, from Kansas City to St. Louis, who would take a collision heading on us and cut in close to read the "Juneau to New York" label. Some wanted to run alongside us. Well, it's a navigable river, open to all. Some wanted to race. Not with old Putt-Putt Dimond they don't.

They were paying for their own props and engines. Our
sponsor was paying for ours, and at my age I'd look silly
telling Big Daddy I had been playing juvenile games and
it cost him money.

I would like to think that we created a scandal that will
live forever on the river. We stopped for the night at
Miami, Missouri. That means we pulled up to the mudbank and Kathy climbed it to go into Miami and find a pay
telephone. Her plan was to arrange with our families in St.
Louis for a rendezvous the next day at Washington, about
forty miles above St. Louis. We would have a rehearsal for
the grand family reunion on the marina docks at St. Louis.
We are what used to be known in the family trade as close-
knit. Kathy's parents and mine, and our brothers and sis-
ters and nieces and nephews and aunts and uncles and all
the other high-ranking officers of familyhood, wanted to
rendezvous on a quiet mudbank before the publicity tur-
moil set in at St. Louis.

There is a distinct advantage, most ways, in being in
Miami, Missouri, instead of Miami, Florida. Miami, Missouri, has a population of 150, all friendly. But all curious,
too. And in the oncoming gloaming of this July day, a
blonde, obviously big-city in her shorts, is traipsing down
the street, looking about. And she hails the first car she
sees. And she smiles, that outgoing big-city blonde way,
and then she gets into the car.

And the Baptist minister takes her to his house. Where,
as the town knows, his wife is not. She's away visiting.

Sinclair Lewis could have made something of that plot
line, given a trifle larger city to work with, for character
population, but Miami, Missouri, didn't. The people know
their pastor better than that. After Kathy had called our
families, the pastor drove her down to our mudbank and
came aboard to talk about boats with me. He seemed quite
at home on the water.

Thanks to the minister and his telephone, we had the
reunion at Washington. We also had a tour of the corncob-

pipe factory. It offends my native pride that people associate Missouri with mules and never with corncob pipes. The mule market isn't what it used to be. The corncob-pipe industry is as strong as ever. We lead the world in the production of corncob pipes, right there in Washington, Missouri. Douglas MacArthur would have been lost without Washington, Missouri. It is unpardonable that children grow up today in Missouri and do not know that their state is supreme in corncob pipes. Why, I was proud to see the factory, which I was seeing for the first time in my life.

It was well that the family met in Washington, instead of at my St. Louis house, the next day. We had planned carefully for the trip. We omitted nothing. We even arranged to have the lawn cut each week. We arranged for everything except to have the boy chained in the yard with the lawn mower. Do you know that during June and July the average suburban lawn in St. Louis grows ten feet high? In pure weeds?

That is nine feet deeper than the upper Missouri River.

"Sweepers, Man Your Brooms"

When our families met us at Washington, Missouri, Kathy and I did not let the reunion get in the way of our docking routine. She turned to and cleaned the *Triumph*, and I gave orders. My mother was indignant. She thought the suffrage movement had been set back a hundred years.

She took me aside and said, "Bill, no husband should order his wife around that way." I laughed and told Kathy that my mother was trying to spring her from peonage. Kathy told my mother that we had agreed before setting out that cleaning the boat's interior and keeping the clothing and the food in order would be her duty. That afternoon at Washington she registered her only complaint, and it was not directed at me but at the Missouri River. The Missouri waters were running a deeper chocolate than usual. Kathy scrubbed the boat's interior twice, with the result that it got dirtier each time. She had a similar frustration again when we were coming in at New York. She had scrubbed the boat twelve hours earlier, at Tarrytown, and it was the shiniest boat on the Hudson, but after it was a half hour in citified water, it was filthy with soot and oil. New York may be a great city to live in, but we wouldn't want to visit there on a houseboat.

I did the hull-cleaning whenever we pulled the boat from the water. That was big of me. I am not the compulsive cleaner that Kathy is. I have been spared a few vices in my character, and getting down on my hands and knees and making love to a floor with a scrub brush is one of them.

However, it is worth going into the practice of good housekeeping on a twenty-foot boat that was home for four months. The authority on the subject is Kathy, since she is the only woman ever to do it, all 8,500 miles' worth. I asked her to give me the rules she set up for herself, and she looked surprised.

She said, "Rules? Why, it's simple. You can't live on a boat like that and have it messy."

Her supplies included a can of liquid concentrate cleaner, a spray cleaner, two scrub brushes, and chrome and brass cleaner-polish. She was so enamored of the cleaner-polish that when we arrived in Key West the *Triumph*'s brightwork looked like it had never met salt spray. Kathy estimates that her average daily cleaning time on the interior deck of the *Triumph* was ten minutes. She wondered, once, if anyone else in the wide world had boat-maid's knee, but I assumed she was boasting.

Getting the laundry done was a continual scramble for her. She sent it out once, at Ketchikan. The professionals kept their record unbroken. They shrank four of her blouses. She was a do-it-yourself laundress the rest of the way, at laundries at marinas, in towns, in private homes. Laundry was a close second to weather as the drag on the *Triumph*'s schedule. The captain would announce it was departure time, and the first mate would howl from the dock, "It's still on rinse" or "It's not dry yet." Our tennis shoes were her special frustration. Bouncing around in the drier, they would spring open the door. Each of us wore out two pairs of heavy tennis shoes on the trip. The *Triumph* was not all that rough on tennis shoes. The laundries were.

Kathy testifies that from Juneau to Key West, as the rivers run and the seas foam, there is only one 30-cent washer-drier. All the others are a quarter for one load of laundry. There is also one free washer-drier, at a marina on the Atlantic Intracoastal, but the drier on it does not work, so she has forgotten the location of that machine. So much for cleanliness, our version of the United States Navy call to order over the bullhorn, "Sweepers, man your brooms, clean sweep-down, fore and aft."

I first heard that from a friend, David Rapp. Dave got out of the Navy in 1963, the year after Kathy and I had met. Early in 1963 Dave and I came upon a relic of a yacht and bought it for $1,000. It is because of that find that I, William C. Dimond, am listed in *Lloyd's Registry of American Yachts,* a onetime *yacht* owner and the peer of J. P. Morgan. Because of that boat I almost did not get registered as Kathy's husband.

Dave and I found the yacht in a boatyard north of St. Louis. It had been out of the water for twelve years. It was named the *After You,* and we let the name stand. For one thing it would cost $150 to get the name changed and a new one applied to her stern. More important, it is the immutable nature of woman to ask a boatman, "Who did you name it after?" and we pleasantly lost count that summer of the number of girls we told, "After you."

She was a thirty-seven-footer, built in 1935. She had a Gray straight-8 engine. Above the Winfield Dam one fine afternoon her gear box departed this world in a glorious burst of fire and brimstone, plus four feet of oil in the bilges. That was after David and I had done something like eight miles of caulking on her seams. She was a streetcar on a hull, and she had a flank speed of eight miles an hour. It cost us $25 to get ourselves in *Lloyd's Registry* with that venerable hog of a yacht, but she was worth it. Kathy says that the *After You* almost broke up our courtship, but she remembers it fondly, too. She put in time on it, both working and pleasure boating on the Mississippi. Kathy and I learned a lot about boating that summer with the *After You.* One thing was especially valuable—we became accustomed to being stared at when on the *After You,* and it helped us become blasé when we were stared at in the *Triumph.*

Which brings up a digression, a return to housekeeping. One reason for keeping a house is the privacy it provides. When one of my ancestors went into a cave after a hard day's work herding the dinosaurs, and closed the bearskin curtains behind him, he could sigh contentedly and scratch himself as he pleased, without causing talk. No such relaxation on the *Triumph*. It was not unusual, on the many nights we slept aboard her, to be awakened by flashlights shining in our eyes. People would hear that a man and wife had given the slip to their keeper at Bedlam and were going from Alaska to Florida in a twenty-foot outboard. So about midnight they would organize a tour, at the marina bar, and come down to have a look at us. The next time we do this I am going to put curtains in the *Triumph*. This time I had to settle for the Dimond Privacy Veil, my shirts and underwear hung from the framing of the overhead, makeshift curtains for the isinglass sides of the tarp.

There are other aspects of housekeeping, of course, that were more intriguing to the casual questioners we met. They would look at the twenty-foot *Triumph*, with its six-foot beam, and ask how we liked being so close, all that togetherness in so little space? Some sniggered, and some were sly, but we like to believe that most people were truly interested and wondered if their marriage could tolerate that much chumminess, day after day.

Kathy and I had an advantage from the outset. My first love was airplanes. I went from model-building to flying lessons in duck-to-water fashion. Automobiles never claimed my attention much. They are the convenient way to get to family dinners or parties or to make sales calls in a city, but they have a way of getting caught in great jam-ups of other automobiles. There is no machine that so much enjoys sitting in great clumps of its kin, waiting for lights to change, for wreckage of unfortunates to be cleared away, and all the while belching nauseating exhaust at the people they hold prisoner, as does the automobile. Kathy shared my armed-truce arrangement with automobiles as an evil made necessary to living today, but she did not share my love of flying. When I was logging hours in private flying after we were married, she would drive to the airport with me. She stayed on the ground, worrying, waiting to hear my voice calling for clearance to land. That was not much fun for her, so it was not much fun for me, and we hit upon boating as a splendid compromise.

We bought a twenty-six-foot Owens cruiser, the *Mary G.* We did not change its name for the same $150 reason that the *After You* was not renamed. I had no idea who the living *Mary G.* was, so that made the name acceptable to Kathy. We sold her not long before we took up life with the *Triumph.* One interviewer asked me if we had a boat of our own and I replied that we didn't, as of the moment, but that we had only recently had a twenty-six-footer.

"Oh, why did you sell it—because you were to make this trip?"

"No, because it cost too much to keep up," I said.

"Would you say that again, please, louder and clearer, into the microphone, Mr. Dimond?" Kathy said.

She has reappraised the economics. Kathy made a long weekend sales pitch, the second or third week we were back in our nonswaying, easily cleaned house in St. Louis, after returning from Key West. She proposed that we buy a cabin cruiser, perhaps a fifty-footer, and live the year-round at a marina in the St. Louis area. On weekends, she said with irrefutable logic, we would not lose the usual two hours driving from city to marina, because we would already be there.

We both became believers in the Power Squadron program and we took its free course in navigation, one hour a week for eleven weeks, and all the homework you can ask. It saved us from watching a lot of bad television. We took the piloting, seamanship, and advanced piloting courses. Kathy had majored in mathematics in college, and after our marriage she had solved the problem of the traveling salesman's wife—what to do while the Roadrunner is away?—by establishing a computer programming business of her own. It paid, too.

Kathy is, obviously, a woman the captain can trust to read a chart while he is working the wheel. That is an asset to compatibility over the long haul in a small boat. A man may lose patience with a wife, but how to quarrel with a thoroughly efficient, quick-reacting sailor?

We talked a lot. We hadn't had as much total time together in the several years of our marriage. The constant chatter was another of the *Triumph*'s built-in kindnesses. The exhaust system, through the prop, enabled us to talk at not much more than living-room volume. We never discussed home or our families, and did not conjecture on what we would do after the trip was over and we had to face the dreary reality that it's necessary to work for a living.

The passing scenery was a major topic. That is standard for tourists. As is standard for husband-and-wife tourists, we do not agree on what is scenic. Kathy likes the fantastic in nature. Alaska's glaciers and the wildness of the Columbia and the bluffs of the upper Missouri were her lands. I like boats, cloud formations, sunlight on waters. The difference in preference had an effect only on the photographs we made. Kathy's are of people standing on docks, waving at us, and of mountains standing behind riverbanks.

She says that her pictures are better because there are so many people in them. I say mine are better because the composition is excellent, the art form often augmented by the action caught in mid-excitement. The time or two when I found the discussion of art-salon photography getting out of hand I would end it by saying that it seemed the moment to take the definitive picture of the entire trip, the one that would bear this caption:

"Now, this is an interesting shot. It shows my wife, a stern view, just after I have propelled her from the *Triumph* in the general direction of the water. She's falling at the rate of thirty-two feet per second, squared, and don't you think that is clever of a math major?"

Revised Sailing Orders: Key West

We left St. Louis on July 25. We headed north from the marina at the St. Louis riverfront, backtracking about fifteen miles on the Mississippi to enter the Illinois River for the run to Chicago. We looked over our shoulders several times, for various reasons.

There was family to wave at, standing on the dock. There was the Gateway Arch, rising 631 feet, a sight that is magnificent. Even Kathy, partial as she is to the high rise of rock bluffs, admits that the Gateway Arch isn't bad, for a man-made structure. St. Louis does have an impressive riverfront history, and there is a quiet and not-much-commented-upon contrast between the arch and its near neighbors, the Belgian cobblestones that surface the Mississippi banks and form the city levee. Those cobblestones knew dray traffic and the footsteps of riverboat men when the steamboat was the marvel of the Western waters. One hundred years ago those cobblestones and the mud-free levee they formed were as grand an advance and as sophisticated a wonder as the Gateway Arch is now.

We were also taking a look at the Mississippi, disappearing around the bend, going its own way some one thousand water miles to New Orleans and the Gulf. I have never made that trip, but pleasure boaters I know who have made it say it is something everyone who considers himself to be more than a dilettante should do once. They never speak of planning to do it a second time. There is heavy motor-yacht traffic going down the Mississippi to Florida waters in the fall and coming back to St. Louis and Chicago berths in the spring. Few owners do their own driving. They hire professional captains, usually with at least two assistants. The captains call the job "running the ditch" and speak of it contemptuously. Plainly, it is beneath their dignity, and they would not stoop to it if the owner were not such a fine, winning man. Such self-sacrificing, river-knowing captains are in short supply, and the yacht owner's winning ways consist in part of the $750 and up, depending on his bargaining ability, that a captain can command for ditch running. The crew comes extra.

The Mississippi is the most difficult of inland rivers, I'm told, and a careless navigator can get lost if he misses a daymark on the lower river. It can also be boring, mile after mile, sometimes half the day long, with nothing but treelined banks. That is not the nature of the Illinois River. Kathy and I had been on it often, boating out of various harbors and marinas in the St. Louis area, but we had never followed it the full distance, to Joliet, Illinois, and then through the Sanitary and Ship Canal, to Chicago.

We had deprived ourselves of one of the most pleasant stretches of boating in the Midwest by not taking the Illinois to Joliet some idle week when we had the *Mary G.* I will say a few kind words about that first, and then come around to the Sanitary and Ship Canal, by way of dessert for indulging my anger at the genius man shows for fouling up his surroundings. We have done so well, polluting the rivers, streams, and lakes, and now we are moving ahead, full of confidence, into the oceans. We have begun with sewage lines out of Miami that have killed marine life in the Gulf Stream off that shore. Another such sewage line is being built at Fort Lauderdale. Of course, everybody is aware of the remarkable success in pollution achieved by the oil drillers at Santa Barbara. Who knows, our children's children may be proud possessors of Dead Seas, covering 90 percent of the earth's surface.

Now, to get off the soapbox and back to the waters of the enjoyable Illinois River. We left the dock at St. Louis with a ballast of pink champagne, a family gift for our wedding anniversary. Even if I were dying of thirst, I'd be reluctant to drink pink champagne, but we had to depart looking grateful. The Illinois quickly soothed us. It is a gentle river, well marked and with a deep channel. Willows and other graceful trees line its banks for a hundred or so miles north of St. Louis. Its waters are relatively clean. Clearing the locks can be a game to try the patience, but the lockmasters are so conversational, sympathetic, and encouraging over the radio that the pleasure boater becomes apologetic in his calls. He really shouldn't be pestering those nice people. The barge captains contribute to the spirit of the Illinois. In clearing the locks, before Joliet, we were allowed by one barge captain to take precedence over his tow; were allowed to come aboard and use his head while in the locks by another; were given a serving of German chocolate cake. The precedence-giving and the cake-giving captain were the same man, met two days and two locks apart. We did not log his name, to our discredit, but his tow was, and we hope it still is, the *Tom Ragsdale*. I believe the line he works for operates out of Memphis.

There were parting shots of grimness when we left St. Louis. Driving to the marina, we were held up by an accident on I-70, or the Mark Twain Highway as it's called in the St. Louis area. The sight of it would be a horror to him, and it was to us. We had been long enough on the river to become estranged from highway brutality, and it made us grateful to be going back to the river. Then, coming up to the Illinois entrance, we saw the Coast Guard dragging the river. Both of us made a guilty checking motion, making certain that those life belts were at hand. I do not know if the Coast Guard was only practicing or had the sad task of trying to recover the result of boating without a life jacket. I preach well, I will try to practice better.

We stopped at Havana, Illinois, the first night up the Illinois River. It was the last of our unsophisticated overnights. We slept ashore in a hotel that could have hung a sign, "Abe Lincoln Slept Here," and not have raised a challenge. If he did, Lincoln ate well, drank well, enjoyed

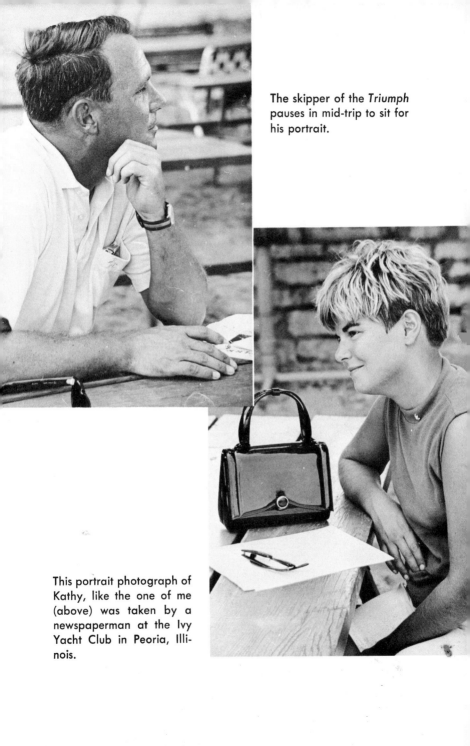

The skipper of the *Triumph* pauses in mid-trip to sit for his portrait.

This portrait photograph of Kathy, like the one of me (above) was taken by a newspaperman at the Ivy Yacht Club in Peoria, Illinois.

a comfortable bed, a quiet night with gentle breezes cool-
ing the room through wide windows, and in the morning
took coffee on the veranda and looked forward to another
grand day on the Illinois River. He did not know that the
Chicago Sanitary and Ship Canal was ahead of him. Abe,
honestly, would have turned about and gone home.

We had an easy run from Havana to Peoria on a hazy and
humid day. The lake that has been formed at Peoria was
being enjoyed by sailboaters, the first we had seen out in
numbers so far on the trip. I gave the sailboaters the
tribute of spending a brief moment envying them their
lazy day of luffing about the lake, then got back to the more
businesslike matter of congratulating myself on being
right on time with the scheduled arrival at Peoria.

Coming into Lake Peoria from the south, we passed the
vast works of the Seagram company. It was the first time
I had seen it, and I had no idea that whiskey-making took
up so much space. The sight reminded me of the comment
that Kathy often makes when passing marinas stuffed to
capacity with large cruisers. She will ask me, "Where does
all the money come from?" not stopping to think that if I
knew where all the money comes from I'd have been there
myself, long ago.

Anyway, passing the Seagram whiskey factory, I wondered where all the thirst comes from to keep it going. I
was ready to contribute my fair share of the thirst for that
day when we docked at Peoria's good yacht club. On a
humid July day cruising the rivers of the Midwest is dehy-
drating. The haze and the heat held for the next day, too,
but the morning of July 28 was splendid. That particular
stretch of the Illinois River, from Ottawa to Joliet, was
another scenic bonus, another day for us to wonder why
we'd had this river in our boating backyard all our lives
and had never taken advantage of it.

The only disadvantage on the Illinois can be the time
required to get through its locks. We had two between
Ottawa and Joliet and were advised that the delay time at

the first lock would be two hours, at the second, forty minutes. However, the amiability of the lockmasters and the sympathetic courtesy they showed us while we waited about made the delays seem almost pleasant. When I get to the gates of heaven and present my credentials, I expect to be detained a bit while my credit rating is checked. I hope the officials at that gate have had previous experience and training as lockmasters on the Illinois River.

When we came out of the second lock, we ran head-on into the heaviest publicity jolt of the trip up to that point. The entire Joliet navy, about thirty strong I estimated, seemed to have upped anchor from the Joliet Yacht Club and come to meet us. The flagship, *The Banker,* a forty-five-foot cruiser, was in the lead. There were two pontoon boats. One of them carried a banner, "Welcome, Bill and Kathy Dimond." It was the largest reception committee we had met, and of course it compounded the enjoyment to see our name spelled correctly on the banner. In my younger years I used to protest that I'm not really a gem and don't want that "a" stuck in my name, but I have almost given up the battle. My lawyer tells me that if I remember to spell it right on checks, that's all that counts.

A fire truck was dockside, to add its siren to the general uproar of bells and whistles sounding on the boats. I was surrounded by boat and engine dealers, a sure sign that they were successful men. I was learning that when we docked at a town or city and found the dealers waiting for us as thick as strawberry jam spread on toast by a loving mama, it was a sign of good businessmen. Fine fellows that they were, none of them told us of the next day's joy, the run up the Chicago Sanitary and Ship Canal. Probably they did not have the heart to do it.

From the entrance to the canal at the Lockport Lock to the exit into Lake Michigan is a distance of about twenty-five miles. I could check that on a map, but I could not bear to look upon that canal again, and it was painful even as a line on a piece of paper. The memories of it are still too

fragrant. An analysis of the canal would show that the top
layer is preowned detergent. Beneath that, surfacing occasionally, is a layer of dead dogs and cats. Beneath the dogs
and cats, too sodden with detergent suds to be able to rise
above the secondary strata of beer cans, are logs. The
temperature was one hundred degrees, which is just right
for bringing the varied aromas of the Sanitary and Ship
Canal to full head. On the bottom, oozing out its exis-
tence, there is about an inch of water, I believe. We were
told it was water. When the natives boast about their local
natural wonders I do not think it polite of the tourist to
dispute the claims, and if Chicagoans like to amuse themselves with the fiction that there is water in their precious
canal, I will leave them to their dreams. We negotiated it
at about ten miles an hour. Several times we were waved
at. The first time, I waved back. The man shouted, "Slow
down." Now we were not making waves with the *Triumph.*
It is not possible to make waves of dead dogs and cats and
beer cans. I suppose he and the subsequent wavers were
only thinking of our pleasure. They wanted us to slow
down the better to enjoy the unrivaled qualities of the
canal. It would have been a lovely point to break up the trip
with a portage.

We lost some interviews in that canal. We were due in
Chicago at eleven in the morning. We arrived at noon.
Radio, newspaper, and television men and a man from *Life*
magazine had waited for us at the locks, watching the
detergent suds flow through, for almost an hour. When we
arrived at the locks—into Lake Michigan—the scene was
bare of newsmen. They knew that canal and assumed we
had been asphyxiated and would turn up, eventually, in the
obituaries. We docked at the Marina Towers on the water-
front, an outstanding repudiation of the canal that was
behind us and evidence that Chicago life can be beautiful.
We made our duty calls at television stations, and in the
afternoon set out for Waukegan. It was our first venture
into wide-open waters since Alaska, and I distinguished

The Chicago Sanitary and Ship Canal, the most aromatic part of the trip.

myself immediately as a chart reader. We were scheduled to be met by the United States Navy at the Great Lakes Training Center.

It was a big chart. Michigan is a big lake. I made a small mistake. Spreading out the chart, filling half the *Triumph,* getting Kathy's confirmation of my peerless navigation, I arrived at an imposing spread of buildings and wondered where the neglectful Navy was, with its official greeters. After bumbling about offshore for a while, waiting for the greetings to start, I pulled in and found that I had steered us to Northwestern University property. There was no opening on the faculty staff that day for a professor of boating, so we shoved off. The Navy had given us up for lost, or just plain no-show, at Great Lakes. If we had a worse day in our four months of publicity-getting duties, I am not going to confess to it.

We came into Milwaukee, the home port of the trip, in sad physical condition. I had a cold, and Kathy had laryngitis. These were the first illnesses that had hit us, and if it had been any other stop, we would have laid up for a day or two to recuperate. But we were to be in Milwaukee on July 31—the only must date on the schedule. Not even weather would do as an excuse. Someone at the office told me when I telephoned the night before and said that the swells were running high and rough, "Don't worry. If we have to, we'll put out a two-mile line and winch you in to the Milwaukee Yacht Club tomorrow morning."

The Dimond luck held. The lake was on its best behavior the morning of the thirty-first, and we were up at 0400. Eager? Pressing to make a good impression on the company people? Nervous because we were going to meet, for the first time, the head of the corporation himself, and make our pitch, head to head, for continuing the trip, going all the way, to Key West? Why, not at all. It just seemed a splendid morning to get up, more than an hour before there was light to steer by, and have several cups of strong coffee. We were due at the Milwaukee Yacht Club

Being interviewed in Milwaukee for television. It was here, at the midway point, that we received our sailing orders to extend the trip to Key West.

at eleven o'clock. We were at the South Shore Marina in Milwaukee at 0830. I never knew a salesman to be penalized for being early, and I wanted to be certain that we would be in position to make that grand entry to the Milwaukee Yacht Club at eleven o'clock.

We did. And at lunch told the company's chairman of the board how well his engines had behaved. They had 219 hours on them at that point, and there was no reason, I implied, that such splendid machinery should be shut down in the prime of life, at New York City. If ever I had met two engines that wanted to race right on to Key West, those were the engines.

He seemed interested. So did his wife. I suppose they went home that night, caught us on one of the several television shows that we made in Milwaukee, and decided that their engines were in good company. The next day we received sailing orders for Key West, and to make certain that we didn't starve on the way, also received the official Milwaukee welcome-visitors package: cheese, sausage, and four cans of beer.

We spent two and a half days in Milwaukee. Psychologically, it was the midway point. We used the time having the *Triumph*'s engines tuned. We also had that porous top fixed, professionally this time. And the clincher in the task of reoutfitting the boat, making it shipshape for Key West, was done by Kathy. She bought two new bathing suits.

Flotsam and Jetsam, True Pals

A number of boaters we met along the way and after the trip was ended asked highly technical questions about our equipment. I wrote an article for a boating magazine on that topic, and some of the points covered then will bear repeating here, just so the mechanics in the audience will be appeased.

The *Triumph I* has a full deep-V hull. That enables her to take anything except a head sea without pounding the crew into hamburger. By reducing speed, even a head sea can be lived through without the crew's wondering why they should go to the bother of it. The six-foot beam I've mentioned before, plus a hard chine, kept her from rolling, while either under way or docked. That is a desirable advantage, when your boat must also serve on numerous nights as your bedroom. She has an extra-high freeboard. That made a joke of the paddle we were required to have aboard in order to obtain Coast Guard certification. Getting the *Triumph* up a creek with a paddle would have been about as practical as digging potatoes while standing on a stepladder. However, that paddle made the Coast Guard happy, and the Coast Guard inspectors at Juneau remarked that the *Triumph* was the best-equipped boat of its size that they had ever seen.

It did look fancy at the dashboard. I've flown airplanes that did not have the high-flying look of the *Triumph*'s dashboard. Each engine had its own electric tachometer. Three electric fuel gauges were installed above the speedometer. Switches on the dash controlled a windshield wiper and a small fan for defogging. Defogging by fan is a nice theory, but it will never replace Kathy, flailing away with whatever piece of cloth comes to hand.

The compass was installed on Kathy's side, to port, because of all the electrical gear that was on my starboard side, and because the steering column acted upon the compass as a magnet. The dual-range, flashing-type depth-sounder was also on the port side. That depth-finder was a constant alarm to Kathy. Once she shrieked, "Shallow, shallow, shallow." Well, she was right, in a fashion. We had been running in water that showed a depth of 180 feet, and the next time she looked at the depth-finder, we were in 90-foot water. High and dry, she assumed. Kathy also had our sixty-watt, five-channel marine transmitter-receiver on her side.

Kathy named our twin engines. They were Flotsam and Jetsam, reading from port to starboard. On the last day of the trip, with almost 8,500 miles behind us, the *Triumph* lurched as we were passing Bahia Honda in the Florida Keys. Kathy was indignant. Jetsam was letting her down.

She said, "That's gratitude for you, we bring it all this way and now it's going to make us look bad on the last day."

The problem was in the gas line. I knew that from a time before, and I told Kathy that the engine really was not being ungrateful to us. I've never been better taken care of than I was by those engines. They were—still are—55-horsepower Evinrude production models. We didn't cheat and use Superwhammo specially made engines. Any boater can go down the street to his favorite dealer and buy the counterpart of our three-cylinder, in-line, two-cycle, long-shaft-model engines. Its features are a capacitor-discharge ignition, three carburetors, and a fail-safe, push-button electrohydraulic shift. The shift locks in forward gear if it's disabled. The engines were given the ten-hour checkup before we left Juneau. They were turning up a maximum 5,400 to 5,500 revolutions per minute then and they kept up that pace until we began going uphill, toward the Continental Divide on the Columbia

River. That tuckered them out, somewhat. The rpm began to pick up again as we came down the Missouri River, fell off again on the Illinois River, the Great Lakes, and St. Lawrence, and the Hudson. When we arrived at New York, the engines knew they were back at sea level and returned to maximum efficiency.

Our top speed at sea level was 35 miles an hour if we were not overloaded with Kathy's spaghetti. Our normal cruising rate was 4,700 to 5,000 rpm, a speed of 27 to 30 miles an hour. That seemed slow for a twenty-footer with twin 55's, to anyone who took only one look at us. A second look told anyone with knowledge of boats that we packed a lot of weight. It was something over 3,400 pounds, including the equipment, luggage, and gasoline. Sitting in the water, the *Triumph* was a deceptive sight. That was an inconvenience to us. When we had to pull her from the water on the two portages in the West, and when we had to pull her for a hull-scrubbing, we had a hard time convincing the resident experts that the *Triumph I* required a tandem trailer.

The full nomenclature for the *Triumph I* is Glastron Gulfstream V-204. She is made of fiber glass. The double hull construction sandwiches a flotation-filled, bulkheaded bilge. Extra flotation was placed in the gunwales. She would float upright if swamped or holed. A tension knob on the wheel could be tightened to hold her on a set course, although the steering system had strong tension without that aid. Both our steering systems were mechanical and were installed separately on each engine, with a connecting rod between the engines. If one system failed, the other would keep us in business, we were told. Fortunately, I must take that on faith. We never had to put it to a test.

Triumph I had three long-range cruising tanks. Two tanks of 24-gallon capacity each were beneath the seats and an 18-gallon tank was beneath the motor well, for a total fuel capacity of 66 gallons. A manual aircraft-type

The U.S. Coast Guard inspectors remarked that the *Triumph* was the best-equipped boat of its size that they had ever seen.

tank-switching arrangement gave us the choice of using each tank individually or in combination. That was an advantage both in measuring fuel consumption and in cutting off a tank of gasoline that didn't seem to agree with the engines' digestion. It happened a time or two. The system required, however, that an empty tank be closed off to prevent air entering the other tanks and their fuel, and until this rather self-evident fact got through to me, I had some puzzled moments. We consumed about eight gallons an hour, at 30 miles an hour, for a cruising range of about 250 miles. The predicted gas consumption had been 4.75 gallons per engine, per hour, cruising. It worked out at more like four gallons per hour, per engine. When we were in Canadian waters, the consumption dropped to about six and a half gallons an hour for both engines, and it was not until the second or third night that I lay awake, marveling and congratulating myself on superb handling of the throttles, that I realized the improvement was due to Imperial gallons, a 20 percent increase in volume over United States gallons. If I'd been paying cash instead of using credit cards, the difference would have been clear to me at the first Canadian refueling. There is a moral in that, but the credit-card people would not approve of having it belabored.

I have previously mentioned that the exhaust system enabled us to talk at civilized voice levels while under way, instead of shouting at one another like Mr. and Mrs. Bickerson. The exhaust system also allowed us to run with full top and side canvas without worrying about the discomfort of having the exhaust trapped in with us.

We did not have the nuisance of dealing with shear pins. The drive-shaft propeller system employs a slip clutch, instead of shear pins. The first time we picked up some seaweed, the slip clutch performed as it had been built to do. The engine raced, and until my slow brain caught up with what was going on, Kathy and I both were in a sweat. It is a grand satisfaction suddenly to realize that nothing is wrong, that the change in pattern is the built-in safety taking over. It is a trifle humbling, but I'm told that is healthy, good for a man's perspective. That may be so. But it reminds me of my mother telling me spinach was good for me.

When we finished the trip, the engines had almost five hundred hours on them. That is equivalent to ten years of use that the average boater would put on them, weekending about on the local pond. That sounds salty, but as a longtime weekend boater myself, I appreciate the versatility of those engines, adapting to varying environments. Early on, you'll remember, I'd told Kathy that water's water, salt or fresh, but if I were an engine I wouldn't really believe that. Spark plugs, to my surprise, were not a problem in salt water. The capacitor-discharge ignition is cool and adds considerably to spark-plug life. I had the good sense not to be my own mechanic, and to leave that to experts along the way. We did not make a spark-plug change until Waukegan, the day before pulling in to Milwaukee, and the mechanic told me then that if I had taken the trouble to wipe the plugs occasionally with a rag soaked in gasoline, he would have been out one sale of plugs. At that, the old plugs hadn't appreciably increased the fuel consumption.

The only do-it-yourself mechanics that was forced upon me was the matter of the gas lines, the source of the stuttering that afflicted Jetsam on our last day and caused Kathy to denounce it. Minute debris in the gasoline would accumulate in the gas lines from the fuel-switching bar to the engines, and in the filters. Twice the accumulation became more than the engine could tolerate, and it began to cut out. It was easy enough to remove the gas lines, flush them out, and clean the engine fuel-filter. It was also easy to tell myself I'd been careless in not doing it before the trouble set in. I feel guilty, now, in not having defended the seemingly errant engine when Kathy upbraided it. My defense is that I'd rather she find fault with an engine than with me, and until heaven improves the nature of husbands, I have a lot of company.

Finally, in the list of things learned while putting those five hundred hours on each engine, are these: The batteries need water occasionally to deliver the goods, and the engines become sulky and go into a silent pout when there is no gas in the tank. Or tanks. Running them wide open, some days for twelve or thirteen hours at a stretch to keep the engines supplied with fuel, seemed the least I could do. So, twice I didn't, as I've already confessed, and if Kathy can forget it, so can I.

"Here Come de Junk"

We left Milwaukee, 4,000 miles logged and 4,500 to go, on August 3. We were booked for the night at Oshkosh, Wisconsin, and that made me feel extraordinarily young again. I suppose that my generation, barely over thirty, is the last that has in the memories of its youth the trade slogan for blue-denim overalls, "Oshkosh, B'Gosh." I wish we could have gone into Oshkosh appropriately dressed, in overalls instead of shorts.

Lake Michigan, some 580 feet above sea level, is not a bargain in boating, judged by our time on it. Somebody in the company headquarters knew that, and we had been told to take several days off at the resort island of Mackinac for rest and recreation. It was four days before we got there. Looking now at my trusty Texaco cruising chart, I can hardly believe that it took us four days to go the length of Lake Michigan in a fast boat. Looking back, I can't help thinking it strange that the opening days of August in a civilized nation should have been so full of rain, fog, swells, chops, and tornado warnings. Fog is the worst. The heavier the fog, the heavier the sound of foghorns on large vessels, the heavier my heart lies in my throat, the heavier my hand becomes, easing back the throttles.

The trusty Texaco map that I just mentioned may require an explanation. It would have to me, anyway, before the trip. The charts that can be bought in marine stores are fine. The charts given away by the gas companies are better, for compactness and a not-so-detailed idea of where in the world of wide blue water you are. Texaco calls its giveaways Cruising Charts; Gulf Oil hands out Cruise-guide Maps; Phillips Petroleum has Cruise Guides. What

I mean by not-so-detailed is that unfolding a yard or two of chart in a cramped cockpit, while trying to keep a compass working for you, can be a terrible nuisance. We had, if they'd been laid end to end, over one thousand feet of charts, or fifty times the length of the *Triumph.* Unfolding those parchments while trying to maintain speed and keep the wheel and the compass heading was a task. The oil-company cruising charts became our standbys, point to point. On the upper Missouri River we used their road maps. We could spot a town name, and sure enough, it would be located on the map alongside a blue line labeled "Missouri River." It was a reassurance that we were on water, or where there was supposed to be water.

We did not take the several days at Mackinac Island that had been offered us. It is at the top of Michigan, a mid-point of Lake Michigan and Lake Huron, and a very proper and social sort of place it is. With fudge all over it. Fudge, you know, can be sticky. So are some of the social strictures laid down in a fudge-oriented society. The Grand Hotel on Mackinac boasts the world's longest veranda. I wasn't expelled from the veranda when I appeared there in my uniform of shorts and tennis shoes and pullover shirt. But dressed that way I would have starved to death. I had to have a coat and a tie to get into the dining room. It was hotel policy.

I had a pair of slacks in a suitcase of odds and ends, in the bow of the *Triumph.* When I broke them out, the slacks had two months' worth of creases, as many on the horizontal as there were on the vertical. Hotel management did not require that a male be well pressed, however. Covered from belt line to ankle filled the bill. Then I borrowed a white jacket from the headwaiter and put on a tie, a four-in-hand. It is the first time I have ever worn a tie on my bare neck, with a sweater looking sort of collar-less lost beneath it. I wore deck shoes without socks. I was not the most elegant diner in the Grand Hotel, but Kathy did say that I managed to stand out in the crowd.

There are no automobiles on Mackinac. Transportation is horse-drawn or bicycles. We tried both. After a mile or so, we decided that we had hired the horse most likely to outdo the entire automobile industry at polluting the air, excused ourselves, got out from behind it, and continued on foot. It is the best way to pick up local lore, anyway. On Mackinac, we learned, the steamers that bring the tourists from the mainland are called "fudge boats." The passengers on the fudge boats are called "fudgies." So we did not buy fudge. On a summer day the population of Mackinac is 5,000. On a winter day the population is 500. I assume the 500 stay inside the whole winter long, making fudge for the coming summer.

When we had absorbed all the fudge culture that was good for us, we headed back to the hotel. Weariness overcame us, and we stopped to have a drink. That compounded the weariness. When we finished the drink and came outside again, the two miles back to the hotel seemed an intolerable distance on foot. We did not want to get behind that exhaust stack of a horse or another member of its family again.

Right at hand, apparently put there for us and waiting, were two bicycles. Everybody on Mackinac has a bicycle. Even the cab men ride bicycles, going to and from their work with the offending horses. Gratefully, we got on the bicycles and rode to the hotel. We parked them in a most conspicuous place, at the hotel entrance. Anyone who knew those bicycles, perhaps had a proprietary interest in them, could spot them immediately. We planned it that way. The doorman was apprehensive.

He said to me, "You'd better not leave the bicycles there, sir. Someone is likely to steal them."

"On Mackinac?" I said. "Oh, no. I'm a trusting soul. Borrow them, maybe, but steal? Never."

We were both relieved when we left the hotel the next morning and headed for the *Triumph* to see that the bicycles were not there. I like the bicycle-borrowing style of

Mackinac. That doorman must be a fudgie himself, a summer import, to speak of bicycle-stealing.

We went into the North Channel from Mackinac. The North Channel is a considerable body of water, but for about a hundred miles it is shielded from the larger bulk and roughness of Lake Huron by the length of Manitoulin Island, stretching east to west in a fetching display of scenery. The next body of water is Georgian Bay, east and north of Lake Huron, and if I could be given a lifetime with August weather in a twelve-month supply every year, I would settle immediately for running out my time in boating on Georgian Bay. We were taking the North Channel and Georgian Bay route to enter the Trent-Severn Waterway at Port Severn in the Canadian province of Ontario, and after our introduction to these social waters at Mackinac, we expected all to be prim and proper. We had no way to be prepared for the junk.

The junk was precisely that, a Chinese junk, made in Hong Kong. I knew that junk-building for the American trade was a Hong Kong business, like suit-making. Several years before, I had read a newspaper story about an advertising man in St. Louis who bought a junk, ordering it by mail, and had it shipped by freighter to New Orleans. From there he brought it upriver and gave it a home on Kentucky Lake. The evening we docked at Cedarville in the North Channel, and saw a genuine Chinese junk sliding up to dock behind us, I thought we had callers from home, the St. Louis advertising man. I am often wrong, but not usually quite so far off the mark as I was this time.

The junk was registered out of New York City. Its captain was not an advertising man, but an actor. He is a specialist of an actor. He has determined where longevity is in the acting business, has settled down in it, and is secure and content. As long as there is daytime television, and women to watch it while ironing, he has a field of employment. He acts in soap operas.

Captain Soap Opera's crew was two college boys and an

unemployed actress. I judge that she was in her early twenties, and in my Midwest innocence I also judged that Captain Soap Opera was along to chaperone her with the college boys. They squared me away on that when they invited us aboard for a drink. The college boys were strictly crew. Captain Soap and the actress were, well, between engagements, she in employment and he in matrimony. It was a fine working arrangement. Kathy, after she got her jaw under control and propped up from the low point to which it had fallen when she first met the crew, liked the jolly junk sailors. So did I. For the next four days we were in touch with them, and it became a game with Kathy and me, competing to see who would first catch sight of that wallowing tagalong and give the cry "Here come de junk."

The actress could not swim, but she had a hair-washing compulsion. The head in the junk did not meet the requirements of her long hair, so she would put on a life jacket, go over the side, and wash her long, long hair in the waters of the North Channel. She did that only when they were anchored or docked, but she could as easily have done it when the junk was under way. There was not much chance that it could outdistance her, in her life jacket. The junk had a top speed of eight miles an hour. Captain Soap said it rode miserably in calm water, and added cheerfully that when the sea was on its beam, the junk was altogether unbearable. It didn't have a wheel, just a tiller. Looking at it, I understood why no Chinese sailor beat Columbus to the disovery of America. We would have outdistanced the junk the morning after that first evening's acquaintance, but we had appearances to make at various stops, and it was an entertainment to be with it for a while. Captain Soap said at one point that he seemed to be running short of cash. I headed that off, before he could go further with me, by saying that we didn't much deal in cash, ourselves, but lived on credit cards. He was not dismayed. He took an old, old issue of a television magazine, yellowed with

A Chinese junk encountered in the North Channel at Cedarville.
A long way from home.

age, from a drawer and sallied forth to do business at a
dockside grocery, paying by check. The old television
magazine had his picture on the cover and was sufficient
credentials for the woman at the grocery cash-register. I'll
never again underestimate the power of a soap opera.

We left the junk for the last time at Killarney, going into
the Georgian Bay. At Killarney we met the General and his
wife. The General is Ralph M. Jerome, a retired brigadier
in the Air National Guard. He and his wife, Lucille, are
from Duluth. When he retired, the General and Lucille
sold their home and all their worldly goods that would not
fit on their thirty-seven-foot cabin cruiser. They endeared
themselves to us immediately by offering us the use of
their shower. We had been sleeping on the boat three
successive nights, and a shower was in order. Ralph and
Lucille were en route to Florida to make their home there.
We were to see much of the Jeromes during the rest of the
trip. That initial kindness, the use of their shower, was
followed by many thoughtful acts on their part. I am glad
I did not meet so winning a general when I was in the Air
Force. He could have talked me into making a career of it.

The Jeromes were taking the Trent-Severn Waterway,
too. It is a unique run, from Port Severn to Trenton,
Ontario. Work on it was begun in 1833, and during the
135 years or so since, it has been the grumble of pleasure
boaters that nothing has been changed, including the lock
tenders. It is 240 miles long, and there are forty-two locks
on the Trent Waterway. It is for pleasure boaters only, and
some of the locks are still hand-operated. However, the
facilities along the shore are numerous and well kept,
many of the locks have been improved, and boaters who
made the passage some years back tell me that the good
nature and hospitality of the lockkeepers is a grand improvement. The Canadian government has apparently
been at work improving the Trent in all ways.

Traffic is heavy on the Trent, and we had been scheduled
to be a week negotiating it. We made it in five days, so I

assume that the Trent has improved two days' worth since it was traveled by the company man who budgeted our time for that leg of the trip. Lake Simcoe, at the western end of the Trent, was labeled on one of our charts, "Caution—Can Be Extremely Dangerous," but it was mild and friendly when we crossed it. We had only two misadventures on the Trent. Both occurred midway through it, at Peterborough. Kathy took a cab into town, in her never-ending search for a hairdresser. The cabbie did not see any of the road. He thought she looked sympathetic, and he spent the ride turning about to address her face to face, instead of impolitely turning his back to her and watching the road. His complaint was business. Both of his occupations were terrible, he told her. Driving the cab was a terrible business, but he had to do it to make ends meet because he couldn't do that on his terrible full-time regular job.

"What's that?" asked my friend the straight man, Kathy.

"Mortician," said the cabbie, almost drumming up fresh trade as he went over the center line.

And also at Peterborough, the *Triumph* was broken into. It was the only time that happened in four months of our journey. Theft and vandalism on boats are supposedly high. All that was taken from us at Peterborough were spark plugs, a bug bomb, and a can of anticorrosion spray. Obviously, some hard-up boater took only what he needed. He would have been welcome to a can of spaghetti, but I don't blame him for leaving it behind. The natives on the dock were apologetic, and mortified that we should have come 6,000 miles only to have our first theft occur at their town. We told them it was a bargain, that their town was so enjoyable we considered it a small price to pay for the privilege of having made its acquaintance. We meant that, but it did not seem to console the towns-people. They were still apologizing, to one another, the last we saw of them.

When we had departed the Trent, and cleared Lake On-

The *Triumph* starts a brief journey overland on the Trent-Severn marine railway in Ontario.

tario, and were well up the St. Lawrence River en route to Montreal, bullhead Dimond had his only experience of running out of gas. Kathy suggested we stop at Kingston, near the head of the St. Lawrence, for gasoline. I said that would be a waste of time. About forty miles later the *Triumph* came to a halt. I mentioned earlier that we were close to shore, and that a dealer came to our rescue. I did not mention then that he was a dealer for a competitor's company, and probably I would not mention it now except that it occurs to me that if *I* don't mention it, *he* will, and have all the better a laugh.

The balance of the run to Montreal was a matter of 150 miles and seven locks. We made it in one day, excellent time, but if one law-abiding, French-speaking lockmaster had prevailed, we would not have made it at all. According to the book, those locks on the St. Lawrence are not for use by customers with boats that are not more than twenty feet in length. I gave our length as twenty-one feet, six inches. It is as easy to invent eighteen extra inches as it is twelve, and I felt safer with that fictional added half foot. The first lock, of course, was the test. If we got through it, we were a shoo-in at the following locks.

Three men were on duty at that lock. Two of them accepted my statement that the *Triumph* was twenty-one feet, six inches long, a legitimate tourist through the lock. The third man did not accept it. He took out a tape measure. The other two stopped him with excited cries of *".Von, non."* They knew that tape measure would catch the *Triumph* short, and I am grateful to them. It is nice to meet government servants who will go along with a little boat-stretching.

Coming in to Montreal, we were getting into freighter traffic. Fond as we are of the reliable *Triumph*, we were never able to overcome the feeling that we were looking a little ridiculous, trying to play the games the big boys do, when we got into the company of oceangoing vessels.

We stayed three nights in Montreal. The first night we

At Montreal's Expo 67. In the background the "Man and His World" exhibit.

spent in a hotel. The next morning we packed and went
back to the *Triumph* and slept aboard her the next two
nights. I was out of practice, staying at a big-city hotel,
being surrounded by men in suits, ties, and polished
shoes. There is a convivial spirit about Montreal, though,
that has nothing to do with modes of dress and propriety.
At the end of the second day I felt myself catching the
Montreal spirit, and I confessed it to Kathy.

"Before we leave here," I said, "I am going to go native,
just once. I'm going to pinch a pretty girl."

"Yes? Well, you better make sure she's a native, too,"
Kathy said. "A tourist might not understand."

The development on that was predictable. Boulevardier
Dimond didn't pinch a girl, native or tourist. Mrs. Dimond, however, riding in an elavator, after the inevitable
date with a hairdresser, was pinched. She did not punch or
yelp. She had gone native, too, and understood.

We had recreation at Montreal, but no rest. We had the
Triumph at the fairgrounds docks. When we turned in
aboard her at night, we had the constant dinning in our ear
of a bullhorn sales pitch to "Come ride to the top of La
Spiral, two hundred and seexty feet in the air." Backing up
that uproar, and carrying on until two o'clock in the morning, was a Bavarian band. And to make certain that we did
not get lonesome, or afraid of the quietness that finally set
in about three o'clock, the garbagemen would arrive on
the docks and throw cans at one another. When we finally
left Montreal, I became confused momentarily and asked
Kathy to check the route on the chart. Bleary-eyed, she
looked at me and said, urgency in her voice, "Oh, for
Pete's sake, just turn right at the first river, and be quick
about it, please."

New York, Are You There?

We reentered the States at Rouses Point, New York, on August 26, and it was a quiet little ceremony at Customs, no fuss at all. I do not remember if I told the Customs officer we had that elephant rifle on board. Probably not. I hadn't seen it in almost three months, and it may be that I'd forgotten about it.

Our first two days southbound on Lake Champlain were rugged. We spent the second night at Shelburne Bay, on board the boat, and that changed the weather. I did not keep a strict count, but after we had been out a month or so it seemed a definite pattern, to me. If the weather was bad, and continued so for several days, and we slept on the boat instead of going ashore, the next day would be splendid. The *Triumph* had secrets built into her that I never did fully understand, but I am grateful for them.

Improved weather was not the only distinction of our night at Shelburne Bay. We met there a boating couple we did not like. Over the entire 8,500 miles, and during the four months, those two were the only people who put a damper on us. They were cruising in a sixty-footer. When we docked, we were invited aboard for a drink. We accepted, the only time that hospitality turned out to be loaded with gloom.

The husband looked like a dropout from a Mafia management course. The wife—well, it was late afternoon, and she was sitting aft, sunning herself, in a flimsy pink negligee. I am not a prude, you understand. It's just that the lady wasn't equipped to bring off that costume with any class. Or much of anything else. Her husband took my mind off her, soon enough.

He said, "Heard about you, damn fools, making a trip like that" and, "What're they paying you, nothin' I'll guess, just like big companies, get a couple of fool kids to do it for the fun and the big shots rake in all the glory" and, "You say you got reservations at what dock? That one? Man, have you been given some lousy advice, they're robbers."

A boy of about ten had come to the docks. He stood there staring at the sixty-footer. He could not have been a native. Shelburne boys have seen bigger and better boats than that. But this sixty-footer was a marvel to him, and with more effort and courage than he had ever summoned before in his ten years, he quaveringly asked our host if he could come aboard and see the boat.

"Hell-no-clear-out," said Genial. He turned to me and said, "Dirty damn kids, let one on he'll come back with his friends. They'd steal you blind."

My drink didn't taste good. I looked across at Kathy. Something was wrong with hers, too. Strange, Mafia-Dropout had told us it was the best Scotch available. Something in the air must have gotten to it. As we left, he filed a parting complaint with me. They had taken the boat to Florida once, he said. Never again. No respect shown them. Everybody there claimed to have seen a sixty-footer, or two, previously. I did a double take, and looked at him, thinking perhaps I had wronged the man. Perhaps he did have that touch of grace, a sense of humor. But he was glowering. He was really angry with all of unappreciative Florida, and he was going to deprive it forever of the sight of his yacht.

The Champlain Canal is a necessary evil. It is also dull, and the men in charge of its operation have bureaucratic righteousness honed as fine as ever it will be done. I would have broken down and complained about it a little myself, if Kathy had not done it for me, and better, in her log. She wrote, "This Champlain Canal is dullsville—10 mph and they time you. If your arrival time at each lock is too early, they hold you up. One crew we heard about was held up for 48 hours. The locks only open at a certain time so if you are five minutes late, you wait 55 minutes. Dull, dull, dull. By the time we got to Schuylerville we were numb."

We started the next day, still traveling the canal, and the service improved. We were let through at two locks, although according to the ground rules we could have been delayed for the better part of an hour. It is not fair to carp at the canal, really. It is the one way to get into the Hudson River. If there is a more magnificent experience in the state than seeing it from a boat on the Hudson, I haven't been advised of it. We were penalized once by ignorance. We passed Hyde Park, but did not find out until thirty miles downstream, at Tarrytown, that we could have visited it. Kathy consoled me. She said it would not have been proper to go calling at the home of FDR in shorts.

One night when we were docked together in the Trent, the General told me, as we discussed the Hudson segment of the trip, that we would not be allowed to go ashore at West Point and make a tour of it if we did not make an appointment in advance. I did not make an appointment, so we contented ourselves by cruising about the docks there. I think the army had shut down for the day. There were few signs of life. The only cadets we saw in the neighborhood were on a forty-foot cruiser bearing the name *West Point.* To the south, at Annapolis, the Naval Academy men were probably having themselves an invigorating twenty-mile hike.

Kathy explained the apparent mass desertion at West Point when, several miles below it, we passed Ladycliff College. "Girls' school," she said. "If you were a cadet, where would you be on a beautiful Saturday afternoon like this?" Off my past record with the military, I have reasonable certainty that I'd be at the Point, walking off demerits. I don't tell her everything I know, though. We ambled on, down the Hudson. We passed the Navy's mothball fleet at Peekskill, and there was a sign put up in the water. I thought it must be something instructional for touring boaters, handy hints on how to store your battleship if you're not going to be using it the next couple of seasons. I had to get within ten yards of the sign before I was able to read its message, "No Approach Within 500 Yards."

It wasn't all that exclusive at Tarrytown. We docked and made ourselves at home in a berth ten feet away from Lawrence Rockefeller's sixty-two-foot *Dauntless.* He is a neighbor of mine, you know, in Lloyd's listing of yacht owners. I would have done the neighborly thing and paid him a call, as one Lloyd man to another, but nobody seemed to be home.

We arrived in New York on September 4. Kathy was nervous. She told me the sponsor's people had been working on this occasion, building up to it, for two years. She told me we had been at work on the execution of it for three months. She told me we had come 6,500 miles. After she had dropped all those news items on me, she told me, crowning horror, that her hair looked a mess. This recital of doom, of course, took place as we were leaving Tarrytown. It sounded bad, I agreed with her, but there was not much else we could do but brazen it out, and go on to New York and act like we belonged there, *Triumph I* and all.

I was as nervous as Kathy was. Bill Pearsall, Mr. Reliable, had said he would have a suit waiting for me at New York. And a shirt and a tie. Then I thought, what about socks? I did not have socks. The board chairman of the sponsoring company would be among the greeters in New York. We were to go to Twenty One. How would it look, Dimond being caught sockless in Twenty One, and kicked out, forlorn and alone on the curb? I spent most of the ride down from Tarrytown worrying about socks. It did not occur to me that somewhere in New York City, there could be a pair up for sale.

We were to dock at the 79th Street Boat Basin. We had been told that we would have no trouble finding it, that it was the only such installation on the New York side of the

Hudson. There was something reassuringly country-directions-giving about that, and I took cheer from it until we caught a four-by-four in one of the props. Kathy yelled. She had known it all along, she said. Five miles from success and all was ruined. It wasn't. I shut down the engines and tilted the props for an inspection. No damage was done.

We passed the George Washington Bridge at 1025 hours and the ever-ready Coast Guard picked us up there, to escort us. Just above the boat basin, we saw the *Chanticleer*, the sponsor's 118-footer. There were about forty people aboard it, waving at us. We waved at them. They waved us instructions to come around again, and wave some more. We did. They waved us around again. I had found my role in life, going around in circles, waving. Finally we got a wave-off, and I pulled up to the dock, where my mother and aunt were waiting for us. My mother was telling three television crews and assorted reporters and photographers all about the perils of boating. Some of them wanted to go out with us and check it for themselves, and since we could not accommodate all of them, the leftovers followed us in a chase boat. I did manage to get us in good company, riding around among the New York shipping. I charted a course past the *Queen Elizabeth*, the U.S.S. *Constitution*, and to a close-up of the *Victoria* being nosed out of her berth by a tug. After that we took our riders back to the dock, then went out to tie up alongside the *Chanticleer*. The wife of the chairman of the board gave Kathy a bouquet of roses, her husband gave me a bottle of champagne. He popped the cork. Expertly done. He took us on tour of the yacht, and Kathy's reaction was everything I could have asked of her. She took in stride such things as a piano on board and color television in the crew's quarters. Well, What else?—sort of acceptance on her part. And then she came to the shipboard delight, the instrument that makes boating a luxury and a thrill, simultaneously—a lovely, full-size, working, gleaming washer-drier. I know what the day of crisis will be in our marriage. It will be the day she announces that we are getting a new washer-drier, to be installed in the living room. I will try to be firm about that.

While in New York we were interviewed by the Today show for television, by N.B.C. Monitor for radio, by *True, Woman's Day, This Week, Motor Boating* magazine, the New York *Daily News, Newsday, Look,* Associated Press, King Features, *Boating Journal, Popular Mechanics, Living Outdoors, Esquire, Yachting* magazine, *Boating* magazine, and *Popular Science.* I think that conspicuous among the missing is *Women's Wear Daily.* They couldn't see a story in Kathy living in shorts and T-shirt all summer. Not a story that would do the industry any good, anyway. We smiled, and meant it, and earned our keep in publicity. It was gratifying. Publicity was the name of the game, and in the immortal words of Leo Durocher or some such statesman, "We came to play." It would have been cheating on our part to accept all the fun of the trip and then become weary or resentful when asked to say a few words into a microphone, or smile, once more please, for just one more camera. We had one telephone call, and a request, that rather surprised us. It was not the nature of the request or the fact that the phone rang that caused the surprise. The call was from the *Chanticleer,* and it was the company's board chairman speaking. He wished us God-speed to Key West, and asked us not to beat him in getting to Florida. That was reasonable. However, it was the first time I'd ever picked up a telephone in the St. Moritz and been greeted by a voice speaking from a yacht somewhere off Sandy Hook. It does make a man feel that he is getting about in the world.

We received a key to the city, but it was not the flattering thing that being telephoned from Sandy Hook was. So many keys to the city have been handed out in New York that it is just a little bit more unusual than being given a franchise to breathe. And we did not get the key firsthand

Our entrance to the port of New York. The ship in the background is also well known for long-distance cruises.

Various relatives, friends, and the press waiting to greet us at the 79th Street Boat Basin in New York City.

At the New York Boat Basin, the chairman of the board pours champagne, and a representative of the mayor's office holds the key to the city at the ready.

from Mayor Lindsay. One of the mayor's men did the honors, and he had a clammy handshake. Disgruntlement, provincialism, is showing through here. It broke out completely the Sunday morning, a week following our arrival, when I awakened at 0630 and said, "To hell with it, this is sailing date. We're going to Key West, starting right now."

The time in New York was a disaster for Kathy, a disaster that stayed with her the rest of the trip in appearance, she claimed, and that will stay with her the rest of her life as an embarrassing moment. It concerns getting her hair done at Mr. Kenneth's.

That was an event for her, every bit as grand as it was to me to be able to go to Abercrombie & Fitch and buy new, lighter sleeping bags. She went into Mr. Kenneth's and said that she wanted a haircut "that will look good when it gets wet."

So the man—not Mr. Kenneth, but Mr. Joe or Mr. Clyde or some such vice-president in charge of transient boaters —assumed that she wanted to try out for the Harvard crew, and cut her hair to an inch and a half. All the way to Florida she looked like a Marine in boot camp, she said. The Marines should have such good luck. Worse than the result of the haircut, though, was the settling of the account.

Kathy had two bills in her pocket. One was a twenty, one was a dollar bill. She charged the haircut. It was $17.50, and that almost destroyed her. She had been prepared to pay New York prices, say as high as five dollars for a job that costs her three in St. Louis. And, sport that she is, she had reached in her pocket, as the hairdresser was almost finished with her hair, and slipped into his pocket one of her two bills.

When she got on the street, staggering with the weight and shock of a $17.50 haircut, she fumbled in her pocket and found it was empty. She knew with awful sureness that she had given the hairdresser the twenty as a tip. Now— admire her—she returned to Mr. Kenneth's and said that she had made a dreadful error, she had slipped a twenty-dollar bill into the hairdresser's blouse pocket, thinking that it was a single. The man smiled, reached into his pocket, and drew forth a single.

"This?" he said.

She received the stunning jolt, then. She had a purse. She opened it and there was the twenty. In the three months we had been boating, Kathy had fallen out of the habit of carrying money in her purse. She had reverted to womanly form, after several days in New York, without realizing it. She mumbled something and fled Mr. Kenneth's, pursued by the humiliating throught that one grimy buck isn't much of a tip for a $17.50 haircut, even if it was one she could have had for free in a Marine Corps boot camp.

All Hail the Intracoastal

I left New York on a typical trash day in that harbor. The pronoun is singular because there had been a desertion. Kathy had gone from New York to St. Louis for a wedding in the family. I had been told by company people that it would be acceptable to them if I took off for the wedding too, but my thick neck was bowed against it. I thought that leaving the *Triumph* would destroy the continuity of the trip. Even if it was never mentioned that both of us had jumped ship for several days to go inland for a wedding, still I would know and that would be sufficient to take off some of the edge. So "I," not the heretofore steadfast "we," left New York, threading through the trash. If it sounds as though I was not overjoyed with Kathy's decision to place a wedding over shipboard duty, then the sound is about right.

Before I had been under way five minutes, I had to stop the engines and kick a four-by-four out of a prop. I recognized that piece of lumber. It was the same one we had picked up coming down the Hudson into New York. Or a close member of the family. New York has an imaginative enlargement on the usual water pollution situation. Every time a large ocean liner comes in, its screws kick loose some piece of a Victorian pier, adding to the junk that just naturally accrues to those waters.

I passed Ellis Island and the Statue of Liberty, went under the Verrazano-Narrows Bridge and into the Manasquan Inlet, then stopped for gas at Bay Shore, New Jersey. I didn't really need the gasoline; I wanted out of the traffic. It was by far the worst concentration of boats I had encountered. I did not know it was possible to get claus-

trophobia on a large expanse of water. New Yorkers drive
boats in the style they are accustomed to in automobiles.
A thousand or so cheerful idiots, seeing the lettering on
the *Triumph* advertising its aim in life, zoomed up for a
gunwale-to-gunwale chat or an invitation to have a drag
race. It was dangerous, and I had to be cautious. The fun
was added to by the quaint practice of many boaters of
anchoring in the channel to do some fishing. On the way
home, they probably park in the Holland Tunnel to have
a fish fry.

My disposition improved when Kathy rejoined me at
Atlantic City. She was full of wedding talk, and I did want
to hear it. I felt a little guilty, and stuffy and smug, about
having put boating duty over family, but I also felt sat-
isfied. Kathy felt a little guilty about having given the wedding priority, so altogether it was an amenable and good
reunion.

Kathy had not been in Atlantic City before. Neither had
I in the summer, though I'd been to sales conventions
there when the boardwalk was under ten inches of snow.
I decided it is better that way. Kathy was disappointed with
Atlantic City. It was not what she had been taught to picture it as, in the Monopoly games. I explained that the
millionaires and their yachts had given up on it a semester
or two ago, and tried to amuse her with an account of
some St. Louisans who started out on the Intracoastal
some thirty years before us. They were Frank Frisch and
Harrison J. (Doc) Weaver. Frisch was the manager of the
St. Louis Cardinals baseball team, and Weaver was the
team's trainer. I do not know Mr. Frisch, and I did not
know the late Doc Weaver, but in St. Louis both are highly
esteemed characters. Characters may be too mild a word
for them, but let it pass. Neither of them will be done
justice until the second coming of Ring Lardner.

Manager Frisch and Trainer Weaver decided to buy a
boat, a forty-five-footer no less, and depart for spring
training in style, from New York to Florida by way of the

Intracoastal. The waterway was not then the improved path that it is now. Even today it has some rough passages, and it always will have. Neither Frisch nor Weaver had ever done more boating than to rent a canoe on the village lake, as a base for strumming a guitar to a pretty girl. But they bought the boat, and after someone pointed out to them which end was fore and which was aft, they set out for Florida. They set the running-aground record for the Intracoastal before they had settled an argument about whether port meant up or down, and starboard referred to the galley or was something that came out of the bilges. They gave up the voyage when it became apparent that at the rate they were going the Cardinals would have completed the season before their peerless leader and great healer of a trainer had made it to some point slightly south of New Jersey. A gray and usually reliable sportswriter in St. Louis, a man who knew them both, says that they abandoned ship the twentieth or so time it nosed into a mudbank, and continued south by train.

"They were going to St. Petersburg," said the sportswriter. "It wasn't until they were buying their train tickets, and saying they wanted to go to St. Pete, that they realized it was on the west coast of Florida, and they were planning to find it on the east coast."

I envied those intrepid sailors, trading in their boat for railroad tickets, when I finally got away from Cape May. The *Triumph* holed up there from September 10 to 14, waiting for weather that would give us an even chance of survival, crossing Delaware Bay. It is a sixty-mile run, and at some points the bay is twenty miles wide. When I did make a run for it, the deciding factor was not so much good weather as light traffic. It was a bruising ride, to the Chesapeake-Delaware Canal. I was out of sight of land much of the time, trying to keep a compass heading with water coming in as fast as the pumps could take it out, and to add to my troubles the windshield-wiper fuse blew. Sixty-footers were playing it safe in some quiet bay. But I had been asking myself, after the second day there, "How long does it take to see Cape May?" and once the *Triumph* had cleared the bay, I pushed on to Annapolis.

Annapolis impressed me as a poor place to train admirals. The tide was out, and I sat for half an hour, with engines idling, just enough power on to control the boat, while waiting for someone to come along and do the friendly thing, catch a line for me. Nobody did. I had to make a four-foot jump—up and away—to the dock. Then the owner of a sixty-footer appeared and suggested I should not tie up there. I wanted to ask him where he'd been while I was trying to find someone to accept a line, but his suggestion that I go away and find another mooring posed an even more interesting question. So I asked him, "Why not moor here?"

"Well, I may be going out before you do, and I might run over you."

He meant it. He was concerned for my welfare at the mercy of his boating. I was not properly appreciative. I said, "Mister, if you can't drive a boat better than that, call me. I can." He looked hurt, and I regretted the remark, but it never ceases to amaze me when owners of sixty-foot boats assume they have three times the privileges and right-of-way of owners of twenty-foot boats. I wonder how they would deal with the captain of the *Queen Elizabeth 2*.

We got around to a necessary overhaul on the *Triumph* at a dealership in Salisbury, Maryland. We pulled the *Triumph* from the water and had the legends on its sides brought up to date, substituting "Key West" for "New York City." The *Triumph* felt better with the record set straight, and she carried us through the Hampton Roads to Norfolk, Virginia, with a fine sense of determination. My determination wavered a time or two during the five-and-a-half-hour run, when water came over the bow. Out of Norfolk, the next leg did not sound cheerful. It was the Dismal Swamp, a forty-two-mile stretch to Elizabeth City, North Carolina.

At Salisbury, Maryland, dealer Ross Lombardo and I check the details of an overhaul. The warmth of the welcome kept me from minding the unwanted "a" that occasionally creeps into our name.

The Dismal Swamp is not dismal. Blueberries grow wild on the banks. We were able to ease up to the bushes, and pick them. Blueberry boating. Juniper and cypress trees dress up the banks, too, but they also contribute a brownish color to the water. It looks like diluted iced tea, but it is not polluted. When we approached it near the Navy yards at Norfolk, I had another encounter with the Navy's penchant for placing major messages on midget signs. When we got close enough to read this one, it declared, "Warning: Photographing, Sketching Punishable by $10,000 Fine and 10 Years in Prison."

My picture of that sign did not turn out.

There was a compensation. Our friends the General and his wife, the Jeromes, were at Norfolk. His picture of the sign did not turn out either. He did get some dandies of the destroyer escorts anchored there. The destroyer escort is a beautifully aggressive looking naval design. They looked mean, just sitting still. He was enamored of them, and his admiration should soothe the Navy, make the admirals feel better about having missed the chance to nab a brigadier general for ten grand and ten years.

I am glad he got away with it because the Jeromes were to provide us with more of their good company on the finishing kick of the trip. At the entrance to the lock of the Dismal there was a sign, "Key West, 1239 Miles—New York, 451 Miles."

For the first time, I had a certain feeling. We had logged 6,900 miles to that point. The numbers on that board did not sound like much distance. And the certain feeling was, we were coasting now, going downhill. Regret came with that. It's inevitable when the end of a good thing is in sight.

Hospitality and Other Perils

The Intracoastal Waterway is the East Coast boater's favorite highway, a Pennsylvania Turnpike with sails and rudders on it. There may be flaws in that analogy, but volume of traffic isn't one of them. I am certain that every boater from Marshmallow Center, Maine, to Lower Chitling, Florida, at one time in his career has a fling at negotiating the Intracoastal. Not all of it, maybe, but enough to say he has been on it and is a member in good standing in the Intracoastal Fraternity.

Kathy and I did not revel much in cruising the Intracoastal. For one thing, we realized that a week before us a few thousand boaters had been along whatever stretch we covered, and that a few thousand more would be coming along the next week. But we could feed our egos on the certainty that nobody had reached it the hard way, from Juneau. Then we had to console one another because the Intracoastal also meant The Ending, to us. After a few days of muddled emotions on that matter, we decided to enjoy the ride. So, at the end, there was only the workaday world, demanding we return to it, but why let that dismay us until it happened?

The Intracoastal has been written about as the most sociable of waterways, a party at every night's mooring, with practice sessions during the day when making shore stops. It could be so if you were all that desperately unselective, but why go to the trouble of running a boat for that? Stay home in the subdivision, and the same gay times will come to you if that is your chosen course.

I prefer to penalize a somewhat heavy head the next morning, and resolve that it won't be that heavy again for some time to come, by waking up on a boat and finding that there is mean water waiting for me. The water is just naturally mean. It stays up all night, taking heady drafts of wind, clearing its ornery intellect for fresh inspirations, and is eager for the games with the boater to begin. In some ways, it is rougher than pulling out of the cozy Roman-brick gateway to Mortgage Manor Subdivision and bulling an opening into the tailgating automobiles. But it is also a natural contest, and I've never yet met a wave that didn't leave the boater a thoughtful interval between itself and the one it was following.

When we left Elizabeth City, we had Albemarle Sound to treat with. Albemarle Sound has been known to break up many a boat. The Sound makes weird waves. It runs east and west, with about a forty-five-degree tilt upward from the west to the east, and it is shallow and has numerous inlets. The combination of these factors produces fallacious waves. They are gang-war waves at times, and attempt to catch the boat from four sides. After all that buildup to the adventures to be found on Albemarle, I am pleased to note that we caught it on a still and lovely day, enjoyed being within sight of low, pretty land and glistening beaches, and had only a rough final hour in the crossing.

Coming into the Alligator River, out of Albemarle, we came to a warning that the Alligator is all choked up on logs and snags. I do not believe in the Alligator River, as such. It is a chamber pot for the Sound above it, not a genuine, working river. We were not quite out of it before we were able to perform our first rescue mission of the trip. A thirty-five-foot sailboat, manned by four young Canadians, had made a wrong turn, angling for the entrance to the Alligator River–Pungo River Canal. A shoal encroaches on the marker, or did that day, and the Canadian sailors had missed, by about two feet, the safety of a ten-foot depth. They realized the deep water was that near, and it did not lessen their supply of unhappiness. I tried to wash them off, with the *Triumph*'s considerable wake. When that easy solution failed, I threw them a line, they accepted it, and I pulled them free. There was no preliminary conversation about waiving salvage. They assumed we did not want to tow them to Key West.

Those Canadians must have been Calgary cowboys on furlough. We met them for the last time at Beaufort, North Carolina, where one of the four had jumped ship. At that less-than-halfway point on a full run of the Intracoastal they so far had been blown out to sea and been taken back to homelike waters by the Coast Guard, had been lost in fog, and had learned enough to marvel at the fact that though every dinghy and seagoing yacht had a radio, they did not. Those fortune-trusting four—or three, now, counting out the deserter—were taking the sail to Miami for the boat's owner. They were making the run for the fun of it, they explained to us. I do not have the psychiatric talent to supply the owner's motives in placing those four lost, lubber souls on his boat and cutting them loose. But I am sure they made it. Canadians always do, somehow.

We had rejoined forces with the General, Ralph Jerome, and his wife, Lucille, and were to continue running with them until we got to the Fort Lauderdale area. The General is a great man to have in any fleet. He is a commissary genius. He is the only supply artist I've met in boating who could go into a darkened small town before dawn and return in ten minutes with hot, fresh Danish pastry. I never questioned the General about his finds; it is best to let the military keep some of their secrets to themselves.

September 24 was Lucille's birthday. The General went to some trouble to provide fireworks for the occasion. We had put in a busy morning at Beaufort, North Carolina, making our speeches about the beauties of seeing America's waterways first, by outboard. The Jeromes shoved off long before we went into our performance. I guess the General figured he had heard it a time or two before. We left Beaufort for Wrightsville Beach and another gathering of the dealer tribe. We did earn our keep on the Intracoastal, putting ourselves on display for the dealers.

Kathy had no more than applied her suntan lotion the way she likes it—too slick for a fly to walk on but not so thick he can bed down in it, either—when we were halted by the Coast Guard. The waterway, we were told, was closed that day from 1300 to 1700 hours. The Marine Corps was holding maneuvers, an offshore bombardment. So, we had blown the afternoon's dealer engagement. The Jeromes had dropped anchor and we tied up alongside them and went aboard their cruiser for lunch and the Marine Corps show. Ralph casually mentioned that it should be quite a show, he'd looked it up in the latest issue of "Notice to Mariners," and had wanted to be certain that he got Lucille there, and the boat anchored, well in advance of her birthday show of shelling.

I just looked at him. He made a manful show of politeness and did not grin at me. Of course, Bill Dimond, salt extraordinary, had not done his homework. He had not read his copy of the "Notice." And had set himself a schedule that had only the United States Marine Corps standing between it and success.

Anyway, the General had arranged for Lucille's birthday afternoon to be spent amid grand salutes of explosions and jet aircraft flyovers. She thanked him for it, and said it was awfully nice of the Marines, too. And those fine fellows, the dealers, when I spoke with them by radio, said they wouldn't mind waiting about for us, not one bit. I have been very good, wherever I've boated from that day on, about reading my "Notice to Mariners."

It is a complaint of people who have cruised the Mississippi from St. Louis to New Orleans that the southern stretches of the run just aren't real Southern, meaning no great white-columned plantation houses lording over the scenery on the riverbanks. The houses are there, all right, but not close enough to the Mississippi for the river to find out about them. The Mississippi would go a mile out of its

way to make a new channel through a plantation-house
drawing room. The Intracoastal has better manners.
There are plantation houses to be sighted from it, and they
are in fine repair, and just any one of them looked like
home to us after all those months on the water. But it is
a funny thing. With all the money that has obviously been
put into those houses, precious few of the owners have
gone to the added, and relatively minute, expense of putting a boat dock at the end of the front lawn. Heaven knows
how much enjoyment they've lost that way, depriving
themselves of drop-in visits by boaters just passing
through on their way from Juneau. An oversight, I reckon,
Colonel.

There was no end to the dealers' hospitality in the
South. There was no end to local pride, either. Local pride
is a marvelously variable thing, and not always predictable.
There is no surprise at finding local pride in architecture
at Charleston, South Carolina, say, but we had to award the
local pride honors for the trip to Aynor, South Carolina.
The Riverside Cricket Farm is located there. It is the
world's largest cricket farm. I have the word of a million
crickets for that, and they were just a part of the year's
crop. In fact, it seems to me that the farm was sort of
between crops, and the million on hand were a low inventory. I hinted some, but nobody gave me a gift barrel of
crickets. I think we must have had a few tins of Alaskan
salmon, and maybe even some of that durable glacier ice,
in one of the lockers. It would have been nice, it might
even have been symbolic of something, to pull the *Triumph*
into her final docking at Key West with a cargo of fresh
South Carolina crickets on stale Alaskan ice. Next time, I'll
plan better.

The hospitality of the dealers brought me down, finally.
I will not go into details of place and time. Somebody
might have told his wife another story about that evening.
Anyway, Kathy had retired, and at three o'clock in the
morning an athlete in the crowd said that his favorite pre-

venter of hangovers was a nice swim in the pool, followed by a workout on the trampoline. Now, he didn't have a pool, and he didn't have a trampoline, but he knew a motel that did. By an odd chance, it was the motel where we were staying the night.

I had a trampoline once. Seventeen years ago. At three o'clock in the morning nothing sounds better than renewing such old acquaintance. So I swam several lengths of the pool and got on the trampoline, and just as I had bounced seventeen years off my psyche, a supporting spring broke. Dimond fell on his coccyx. Now I am pointed on only one end, my head. I did not get to bed that night. I stayed up, moving about, certain that my legs were paralyzed but had not yet received the message. The Coast Guard would have been proud of me the next three days. Not once did I sit down on the *Triumph* without first making certain my life preserver was beneath me.

Kathy was appreciative that I had regained sufficient coccyx dignity to walk more or less upright and with some sign of confidence in staying that way by the time we got to St. Simon Island, just north of Brunswick, Georgia. St. Simon was our one sentimental port of call. The sentiment was once removed, but important, in a family way. My mother and father spent their honeymoon there, and they stayed at The Cloister. So Kathy and I stayed at The Cloister overnight. I could not carry my load of sentiment into the dining room. Gentlemen are not permitted there in Bermuda shorts, no matter how noble their sentiments. I guess my mother forgot to tell me that. Anyway, the sentiment was cut short, to about a seven-hour stay, because of the press of dealer appearances. I paid $58 for the seven-hour display of sentiment. My mother forgot to tell me about the rates, too. I suspect my father's sentiments, as he reached for his wallet, were the same as mine.

On the Intracoastal the palm trees become part of the scenery not much south of Savannah. And in Florida, at Jacksonville, there is the splendor of the water hyacinths

In Florida at last, we examine our course from Miami to Key West.

choking the St. Johns River, and in the air there was a very special Welcome-to-Florida flu. Jacksonville boaters are the only ones privileged, in the national game of claiming home waters as the most dangerous, to decorate their horror stories with flowers. I do not recall much about Jacksonville's water. The flu was taking over fast. I do recall that a dealer pointed out a spectacular building and told me that the top of it went around. It was not in the going-around league with my head. Kathy took over the boat driving for a day or two, and that north-Florida stretch of the Intracoastal is memorable to me mainly because of the flu and St. Augustine. The Spaniards left a splendid fortress there, and the merchants and city officials are working on an even more splendid monument to their good taste. They are doing away with neon signs. There is no other sight like it on the Intracoastal, or even in the Mojave, perhaps. It is the only town of any size where I can recall standing on Main Street and looking about and feeling elated that something was missing. The neon jungle growth.

We stopped at Jensen Beach, and the sponsoring company's board chairman seemed grateful that we had been polite, and had not beaten his yacht to Florida. It seemed the least we could do.

It was the first week of October, and the Miami-to-Nassau race was coming up. I said it would be a thrill to enter that. Surely there would be an opening for the *Triumph*. In fact, I was certain of it, in the under-200 class, and we would be a lucky-Dimond cinch to win it. We would have, too. No other boat had entered it. I believe the matter was dropped with one look, chairman of the board to Dimond. While we were in Miami, I met many of the drivers of the big boats, the ones that get up on the steps and have an area about half the size of a paddle in the water when they're under full power.

One driver told us he had the best-knit physique in the world. More than two thousand stitches. He seemed a

The traditional fireboat welcome to Key West.

Cruising in to Key West, just ahead of an impending hurricane.

truthful man, too. Another had lost an arm to the sport. All
of them had pearly smiles. False teeth. The Coast Guard
approves of this pounding, difficult race, the drivers said.
It gives the Guard an opportunity to train personnel under
controlled conditions. Why, in the usual run of luck, said
the drivers, they will give the Coast Guard all the sinkings
and capsizings they need to train a new batch of seamen
in rescue work.

There were two heavy letdown thuds on that finishing
run from Miami to Key West. It isn't much for distance,
about 151 miles, but it is tricky—about like the Missouri
with rocks and sharks in it, so far as opportunities to
ground a boat are concerned. However, I will admit that
while I will take the Missouri for forgiveness, in the matter
of running aground and letting you off to try again, I will
take the Florida Bay for color. Blue-green water is more
natural than brown, somehow.

The first thud occurred on October 9. We docked at
Marathon just in time to catch the demise of the St. Louis
Cardinals in the World Series. The dealer who greeted us
at the dock said it was a great day in his life, meeting two
St. Louisans just then. Hadn't been so happy about anything since he'd left Detroit, still nursing a boyhood
grudge against the Cardinals for beating the Tigers and
making the Depression of the 1930's extra unbearable. So,
some thirty years later the Tigers had their evens, and he
made us very comfortable at Marathon.

The second thud occurred the next day. It was my
birthday. Never trust a man over thirty to enjoy another birthday.

Weather was building, the morning of October 11, and
for several days it had been suspected that a hurricane was
in the offing. That did not deter the United States Navy
from making an occasion of our arrival at Key West. A
fireboat was there, pumping water for us, just in case we
had not seen sufficient water.

On the dock there were sailors and officers in full whites.

Our last chore of the trip, passing a line to secure the *Triumph* at Mallory Square in Key West.

I'm feeling a little pensive at the end of our 8,500-mile outboard odyssey.

The last haul of the trip. The *Triumph* is lifted from the water upon completion of the longest voyage of its kind.

I brought the little *Triumph*, the modest and durable and uncomplaining *Triumph*, to her final berthing of the trip, and looked at all those good Navy men stretching out their hands to accept a line. I passed up four commanders. They would not do. I took the line in hand and threw it to a fifth man.

He caught the line and made us fast, in a swift and knowing handling. It was a fitting piece of seamanship to end the 8,000-plus miles, and we thank you for the tie-down, Rear Admiral F. J. Brush.

Epilogue

We had a reentry problem. That should not surprise anyone. Mine was to go back to work, in an office, and in mid-November 1968, I went to work in the sponsoring company's office at Milwaukee. That hasn't much shock value, either, but it really was not until we had reached New York that the company people became firm in their talk on the matter, and that I began to look at boating as a career instead of a weekend off from selling folding doors.

I am still a salesman, although by title I'm sales promotion and training manager. As a salesman, I am infatuated with statistics. Bear with a few, please: Pleasure boating is a $3.15 billion business in boats, motors, and service. There are 8.5 million pleasure boats in the United States, and nearly 7 million of them are outboards. Four manufacturers of outboards—Evinrude, Johnson, Mercury, and Chrysler—do 98 percent of the business, and all are located in Wisconsin.

The statistics I've given impress me, but I am even more impressed by the embryonic aspect of the outboard-motor industry. It has been only in the past few years that outboard motors have been made sufficiently powerful to take the likes of the *Triumph* into open waters, to trespass on whales' territory. For some sixty years the outboard was for the man who wanted to keep company on some quiet lake with bluegill. No longer.

Market analysts have a term for what prompts the sale of larger, more powerful, better engines, and the term is "performance image." It used to be called Keeping Up with the Joneses, when our company was founded in 1909. The founder built a 1.5-horsepower engine that sold for

$62. His wife, Bess, wrote the advertising copy, and she knew how to get around a wife who couldn't see the wisdom in spending all that money on a contraption. Her promotion copy read, "Don't Row! Throw the Oars Away!" How could a woman resist the vision of getting that far ahead of the neighbors, on Lake Gitchi Gumee?

The founder didn't try his first motor on Gitchi Gumee, but on Lake Pewaukee, which has almost as improbable a name. Kathy and I live not far from Lake Pewaukee, in Pewaukee, Wisconsin, on the lake's shores. We have gradually, with the assistance of postmarks on letters, convinced our relatives and friends that we are not being earthy about Milwaukee, and that it does have a neighboring town of several thousand, Pewaukee. And very nice it is, too, in Pewaukee.

In the summer Pewaukee is a resort town. In the winter it is a village, with iceboats and skaters on the lake, and Kathy and I are fake farmers, living in what was once a farmhouse on a dairy farm. It is like no other farmhouse I have met. It was built by a manufacturer of heavy machine equipment, used in coal mining. We rent it. And as I sit here in my study ... Well, how many farmhouses have studies? Finding the farmhouse for rent was a stroke of luck, and perhaps it was the *Triumph* at work. We bought the *Triumph*. We wanted it near us. And it is—in a barn where the machinery was once housed to do whatever work needs to be done around cows.

She is well cared for, the *Triumph*. When she makes personal appearances at boat shows, she often, and properly, receives more attention than we do. At such public appearances there is a large display board, detailing the route of the *Triumph*. Standing beside her, I have seen people look at the *Triumph*, and then at the photographs of Kathy and me, and say, "I wonder if they had a good time?"

Yes.